Bold & Brilliant
Phyllis Sloane's Pop Portraits

Presented by: ARTneo
@ 78th Street Studios
1300 West 78th Street | Cleveland, Ohio 44102

June 20 - August 24 2014

Curated by Christopher L. Richards

Lenders to the Exhibition:
Phyllis and Bob Lester
Rachel Davis Fine Arts

Published by ARTneo, Cleveland, OH

Introduction by Laura Dowler
Essay by Christopher L. Richards
Edited by Christopher Busta-Peck and Louise Mooney

Design: Christopher L. Richards
Photography: Christopher L, Richards
        Fig. I courtesy of Phyllis Lester
        Portrait of Phyllis Sloane by Newson Shewitz, c. 2000, courtesy Ginna Sloane
        Photograph of Morjorie Talalay and Nina Sundell courtesy of MOCA Cleveland

© Copyright 2014 ARTneo: the museum of Northeast Ohio art and architecture
17801 Detroit Ave Cleveland, OH 44107
www.artneo.org

ARTneo programming is made possible by memberships and through support from:
Cuyahoga Arts and Culture, the Ohio Arts Council, The Cleveland Foundation,
The George Gund Foundation, and The David & Inez Meyers Foundation.

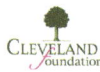

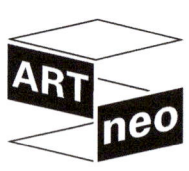

the museum of Northeast Ohio
art and architecture

Acknowledgements

One of the first Cleveland artists I became aware of when I returned to the area after completing my Bachelor of Arts in Art and Design at LaGrange College in Georgia was Phyllis Sloane. The very first image I saw of hers was a print of a woman beside a changing screen with clothing hung from it. I was immediately struck by the flatness of the image and sought out more information about her. It was a great pleasure to find such a large quantity of her work (a majority of which was given by the artist) at the Cleveland Artists Foundation when I began working on photographing the collection in 2011. At that time, the initial thoughts about this exhibition began to solidify. So many of the pieces showed a relationship to Pop Art. Lauren Hansgen, then executive director, encouraged me to continue to develop the idea with the possibility of presenting the exhibition.

That opportunity has finally arisen. Presenting this material after the organization changed its name to ARTneo is perhaps perfect timing. Phyllis Sloane is not often linked to Pop Art, and to make such a case shows ARTneo's ability to expand its scope and examine untouched areas of Northeast Ohio's artistic history. This exhibit is also a celebration of ARTneo's collection with the majority of the works coming from its holdings. Without the support of Joan Brickley, President of the Board, and John Farina, Interim Executive Director, this exhibit would not have been possible. The ability to present this exhibit is a result of the support and assistance of many individuals. I would like to sincerely thank Dan Bush for providing ARTneo with an exhibition space art the 78th Street Studios, Peter Iversen and Rachel Davis for helping secure temporary walls, and Shaun Edwards, who helped to install said walls. Gratitude goes to Ginna Sloane for her correspondence and enthusiasm. Special thanks to Christopher Busta-Peck for his assistance in many aspects of this exhibition, as well as to Laura Dowler for writing a biography for this catalog. Finally, I would like to thank the lenders to the exhibition, Phyllis and Bob Lester, who graciously allowed me to view their collection of Phyllis Sloane's work, and Rachel Davis Fine Arts.

- Christopher L. Richards

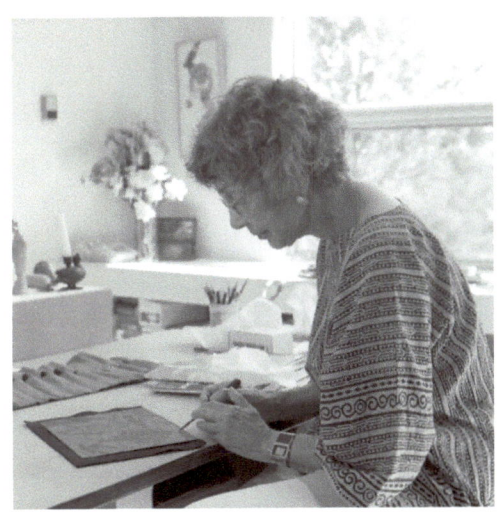

Phyllis Sloane, Newson Shewitz, c. 2000, courtesy Ginna Sloane

Introduction:
Phyllis Sloane (1921-2009)

Laura Dowler, MLIS

Phyllis Sloane was born in Worcester, Massachusetts, in 1921. Her family moved several times when she was growing up, but eventually they settled in Cleveland. Sloane's first artistic success was as the winner of a poster contest in the 5th grade. This was only the beginning for Sloane who would go on to have a major influence in Cleveland art. She graduated from Cleveland Heights High School and attended Carnegie Institute of Technology (now Carnegie Mellon Univeristy) where she earned a BFA in Industrial Design. After college, Sloane did freelance product design in New York and Chicago and then started PDA Design Company in Cleveland with Newson Shewitz and Anthony Vaiksnoras.

Sloane left PDA in 1949 to raise a family, but leaving her job did not mean leaving her art. She found other female artists (generally consisting of Sloane, Elaine Cohen, Dorathee Manbeck, Algesa O'Sickey, and Phyllis Seltzer) who would meet regularly to practice figure drawing and share each other's company. In 1959 her work took on another facet when she acquired an old printing press. Sloane rebuilt the machine and began to experiment with screen prints and lithographs with no formal training in those media. Her early work has a very abstract style, but she would soon find influence in the figurative and Pop artists of the 1960s.

Throughout the 1960s and 1970s she would focus on the female figure as her subject. She captured the female figure using a variety of media and in a style that was uniquely hers. She told Kate McGraw from the *Albuquerque Journal* in 2007, "I never leave the heads out. Many artists do; they're only interested in the body. I'm always interested in the person. There are some models I've used over and over, because they fall into wonderful poses." Some of her subjects have included Edris Eckhardt, Berenice Kent and Marjorie Talalay.

In 1978 Sloane purchased a house in Santa Fe, New Mexico. This area would have a profound impact on her life and art. She spent summers there, built a studio there, and eventually, in 2003, she left Cleveland and made Santa Fe her permanent home where she was close to her children and grandchildren.

During the 1980s and 1990s the subject of Sloane's art shifted from the female figures to objects. She created many carefully arranged still life paintings and cityscapes. In recalling the cityscapes she told the *Las Vegas Sun*, "It was a mood that reached me. It was like discovering a whole new world for me, like the way I felt when I went to Santa Fe and saw the landscapes." Sloane was an artist who was always discovering and experimenting with various modes of artistic expression.

Sloane's work was celebrated throughout her career. She was the 1982 recipient of the Cleveland Arts Prize for Visual Arts, and her 1996 exhibit at the Mansfield Art Center resulted in the publication of *The Art of Phyllis Sloane* by H. Daniel Butts. She exhibited over twenty solo shows, and in 2004 she was honored with a retrospective at the Las Vegas Art Museum.

Sloane remained active as an artist for her entire life. In 2007 she told Kate McGraw from the *Albuquerque Journal*, "It's a blessing to have work you love and feel no need to 'retire' from. There's always something that helps keep you really interested. It's wonderful to have something I've been able to do my whole life. I think most artists feel that way." Two years later, in 2009, Phyllis Sloane died at the age of 87 in Santa Fe, New Mexico.

Consuming Figures

Shifting the Vocabulary of Pop Art

Christopher L. Richards

The term Pop Art has been applied to a number of artists who worked during the 1960s and 1970s. Art historians have attempted to create a definition of qualities that define Pop works of art. Generally, Pop paintings were representational, making use of existing imagery, stressing two-dimensionality with the emphasis on flatness and frontal presentation. Centralized compositions were commonplace, and flat areas of color with hard edges informed an inexpressive style that removed the artist's hand. With these artists and works there was a general sense of the decorative and kitsch. Commercial art as a source emphasized such decorative qualities.

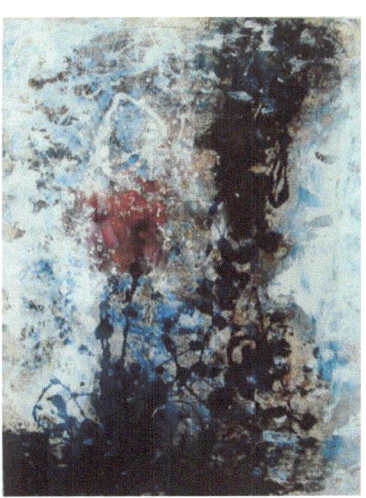

Fig. 1. *Untitled* [Action Painting], 1959, acrylic on paper. Collection of Phyllis and Bob Lester

Like many Pop artists, Phyllis Lester Sloane began in the commercial art field working in industrial and graphic design. Having earned a Bachelor of Fine Arts in Industrial Design from the Carnegie Institute of Technology in 1943, Sloane pursued a career in design at Sears, Roebuck & Co. in Chicago, and at the architectural department at Oklahoma A&M University. After holding freelance positions in New York City, she returned to Cleveland and opened a design firm, PDA (Packaging, Design, and Advertising), with partners Newson Shewitz and Anthony Vaiksnoras in 1946.

Art critic Helen Cullinan wrote of Sloane's 1974 exhibition, *Women*, that "something in the artistic process of this artist produces pure design, flights of line and flat areas against detail and pattern."[1] This pure design is reflected in Sloane's own enjoyment of creating the work, "What excites me most is the breaking up of the space."[2] Though much of Sloane's work reflects this design background, her works are not often seen as having commonalities with Pop Art. A great majority of her work speaks to her own artistic vision, which lies beyond any particular movement.

Pop influences do appear in her paintings and prints of the 1960s and 1970s. The Pop style emerged in the early 1960s and was quickly seen as a challenge to Abstract Expressionism. The artists reveled in the idea of creating a fine art that spoke to the lowbrow culture of the general public, but was not a movement in the common sense of the term. Pop artists did not form groups; nor did they publish manifestos. Pop Art became a reflection of the era in which it was produced. It was youthful, a symbol of consumerism and cultural turbulence, during a time when people enjoyed more opportunities with increasing wages and affordable mass-produced products that allowed for a higher standard of living. Change also came in the form of social issues, such as the Equal Rights Movement, the Women's Liberation Movement, anti-war protests, and the sexual revolution.

1. Helen Cullinan, "Art & Artists," *The Plain Dealer*, December 19, 1974, 11-E.
2. Kristen Peterson, "No Sloane Down: At age 83, artist still works in multiple mediums," *Las Vegas Sun*, July 22, 2004, http://www.lasvegassun.com/news/2004/jul/22/no-sloane-down-at-age-83-artist-still-works-in-mul/.

Sloane abandoned Abstract Expressionism [fig. 1] early on, turning toward the figure as subject matter, which was at the time a fairly unpopular move. Many artists in the late 1950s and early 1960s were criticized for returning to figurative painting. In what was termed "New Realism" –a broad category of art consisting of contemporary figurative painting– Philip Pearlstein had been accused of being too academic. Pearlstein rejected that idea, stating that "It's impossible, because the academicians work by rules, not by vision. I construct the whole thing out of visual measurements."[3] Alex Katz, who also moved away from Abstract Expressionism early in his career, began his figurative paintings during the development of Pop Art. Though he did not employ the strategies of Pop Art's use of mass-produced consumer goods and media, his work, similar to Sloane's figures, relied on a visible reality and the reduction of the figure into an iconic image using flat planes of color with hard edges. Both Sloane and Katz became concerned with a visible reality and its translation into an object housed in pictorial artificiality by creating a simplified metaphor that represents the people in their works.

Sloane goes further in the abstraction of her sitters than other New Realist artists and enters into the Pop Art category. Pop portraiture makes use of signs that represent an individual's identity in the popular public consciousness. Components of glamour, fashion, excitement, affluence, and a fascination with fame form the basis of portraiture in Pop Art. Pop artists made use of media to create images not to examine just the superficiality that creates celebrity was made, but also to examine the real person. Recognizable personalities are not always the subject of figurative works in Pop Art. Several artists, such as Tom Wesselman and Allan D'Arcangelo, obscured the identity of their subjects. Figures being represented were drawn from life rather than from utilizing appropriated images. The seemingly anonymous figures in Pop portraiture respond to the status of the individual average person in a modern world that exalted the mass produced over that of the handmade and unique.

Sloane's portraits have an interplay of likeness and unlikeness, "I never thought of them as being strictly portraits. I always thought of them as figure paintings, although I did want to get a likeness."[4] She examines both public and private identity, and she employs popular fashion and pattern to create reductive forms with positive/negative space reversals. Using only the first names of her sitters as the titles of the work begins to explore the idea that traditional portrait artists viewed identity as timeless. At the same time use of these titles acknowledged that recognition of the sitter is subject to temporality, or access to well-documented biographies. Only the individuals who were living during the lifetime of the sitters, and perhaps only those who personally knew them, will recognize and recall their identities without the assistance of historical documentation. This illustrates the paradox of portraiture as an art form as Sloane created works that grasped the essence of the identity of an individual that lies in temporal reality, while simultaneously creating a valued and independent work of art after the sitter is no longer identifiable.

Further, the use of only a first name as a title challenges the uniqueness of an individual. Paired with the surname, a given name is supposed to set people apart. It distinguishes individuals from others, emphasizing a thier specificality. The appearance of a

---

3. Ellen Schwartsz "A Conversation with Phillip Pearlstein," *Art in America*, September/October, 1971, 55.
4. H. Daniel Butts, III, *The Art of Phyllis Sloane* (Cleveland: Ohio Artists Now, 1996), 15-17.

given name solely as a title to portraits emphasized this singularity while at the same time denying it. Many portraits of Sloane's are of seemingly anonymous subjects. Works like *Rose* [fig. 2] give the viewer a sense of a person's personality. Without the context of who the person is, the figure shifts into a representation of an average generic human being.[5] In this way, it reminds the viewer that through popular fashion and mass-production, there is a loss of specific identity.

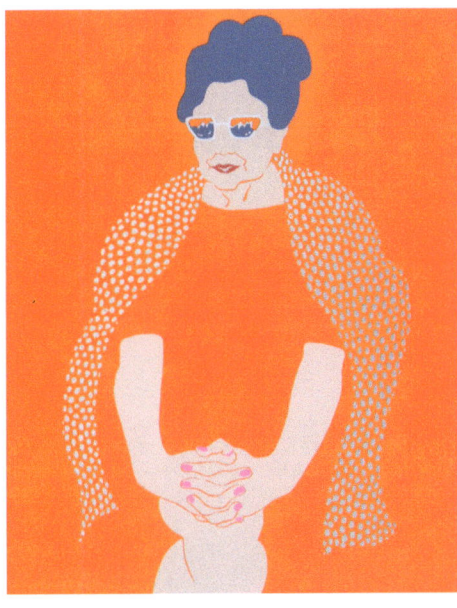

Fig 2. *Rose*, 1970, screenprint on silver posterboard, 22.5 x 18.5 in. ARTneo Collection, Gift of the artist, 2002-815

This loss of identity directly relates to the Pop fascination with fame and its often fleeting status on the individuals upon which it has been bestowed. Portraiture in Pop Art was a means to explore the concept of celebrity. When Andy Warhol stated that Pop Art is about "Liking things" and as other critics placed greater emphasis on the idea that Pop consisted of still lifes of mass-produced consumer culture, they confused the public that the movement was more about objects than the human form. Paul Moorhouse writes that this perspective "fails to account for the rich complexity of images of people which characterizes the iconography of Pop. This is surprising, and also anomalous given that most critics recognize Pop's preoccupation with scrutinizing the nature of and language of consumer culture, yet they ignore the fact that portraiture is a vital part of that scrutinizing process."[6] Warhol himself relied heavily on portraiture in his work: some of his iconic and widely recognized works being portraits of celebrity figures of Jackie Kennedy and Marilyn Monroe. Pop artists became interested in the human aspects of a consumer driven society and how individuals gained almost instant fame from being presented in film, newspapers, and advertising. This created a sense of loss in personal identity and the creation of a publicly held character.

Sloane's own subjects often had celebrity status in Cleveland as personalities in the local arts scene. Some, like Berenice Kent and Edris Eckhardt had nationwide reputations. While Sloane did not engage in the critique of how her sitters became so well known, she did utilize both their public and private personas to inform her depictions of them. Many of her subjects became well known through appearances in the media. Eckhardt had a regular appearance on a television show in the late 1940s where she worked on sculpture in front of two actors. Kent enjoyed a constant presence in the local newspapers. The press has been one of the most influential media in the creation of celebrity and social status, as Willis B. Inman noted, "There are few sources that suggest social position in community life more forcefully than those found within the columns of the society section of a newspaper..."[7] Examples of Sloane's use of public and private identity

5. Rose was Phyllis Sloane's oldest sister. Ginna Sloane described her aunt, "Rose was always very well dressed, well 'put together'. She had long hair her whole adult life (when I knew her) that she put up in a bun. You see that in this silkscreen. Also she loved high heels. When I was young and visited her, I loved to play dress up in her closet and put on her high heels and furs.

   "She was a very loving aunt. Once in the sixties, I bought her a tube of lipstick that was fire engine red (at the time pale shades were in vogue). She wore that red lipstick anyway–she was open to her niece's taste!" Ginna Sloane, email to author, May 19, 2014.
6. Paul Moorhouse, *Pop Art Portraits* (New Haven: Yale University Press, 2007), 45.
7. Willis B. Inman, "The Semantics of Social Status on the Society Page," *The Clearing House*, Vol. 42, No. 9, May, 1968, 560.

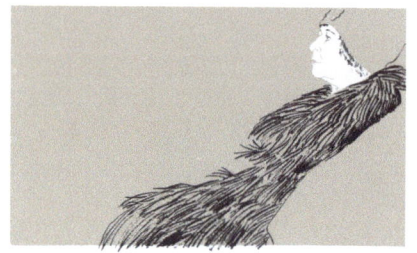

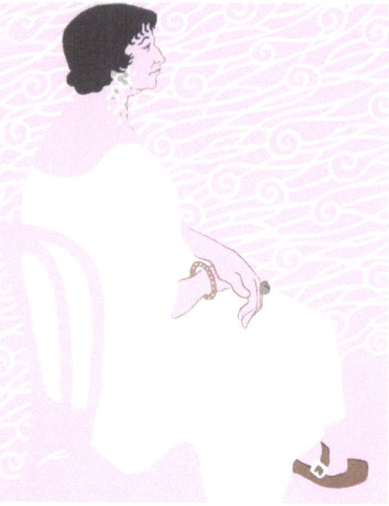

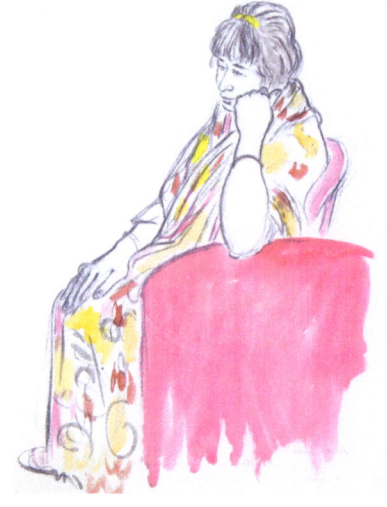

Fig 3. *Berenice*, 1969, screenprint on paper, 11 x 18 in. ARTneo Collection, 1986-254

Fig. 4. *Berenice*, 1969, screenprint and mylar on paper, 22.75 x 18 in. ARTneo Collection, 1986-283

Fig. 5. *Berenice Kent*, 1970, charcoal and watercolor on paper, 25 x 20 in. ARTneo Collection, Gift of the artist, 2002-809

are manifest in the portraits of Berenice Kent. They reflect this concept most clearly when viewed together.

Widely known as the "Art Deco Queen," Kent came of age in the era of flappers, and devoted her later years to lecturing on and dealing in the decorative arts of the period. In 1972, her apartment filled with Art Nouveau and Art Deco decor was packed up and shipped to Texas to create an authentic display for the Texas State Fair. The theme had been the *Dazzling Thirties* to celebrate the era in which the buildings had been constructed. Beyond lending the contents of her apartment to a state on the other side of the country, Kent's local reputation was that of a wild and carefree eccentric. Her name regularly appeared in the newspapers, often times not really having anything to do with the topic at hand. Her personal fashion sense was constantly described, whether the article warranted going into those details or not.

Kent's overwhelming popularity in Cleveland culminated in a 1978 exhibition at the Butler Institute of American Art in Youngstown, Ohio, of nearly fifty portraits depicting her image by different artists. Clyde Singer remarked "It's some kind of 'fun' show and there can't be any like it floating around these days."[8] Indeed, the repetition of Kent's likeness held in one exhibition could be viewed as a work of Pop Art portraiture itself. Singer goes on to say "...it's a case where the over-all, or theme, is far more important than the singleness of individual efforts."[9] Sloane had contributed four portraits to the exhibition, and had created many more.

One portrait in the exhibit was titled *Monkey Fur Coat*. It was a screenprint of Kent in profile, officially titled *Berenice* [fig. 3].[10] The print shows Kent in an elegant and poised posture while simply and subtly expressing her taste in fashion through the use of black line on a taupe background. It is a rather understated, yet stately depiction of the "Art Deco Queen." A second print titled *Berenice* [fig. 4] from 1969 shows Kent in profile again. The form of her dress is reduced to a hard-edged white shape on a pink background with an Art Deco surface pattern. While here her wardrobe is simple, Kent's

8. Clyde Singer, "'Flapper' Age Comes To Butler," *Youngstown Vindicator*, January 22, 1978 (ARTneo Clipping File, "Phyllis Sloane")

9. Ibid.

10. It is possible that Berenice Kent preferred a more expressive title. *Monkey Fur Coat* appears as the print's title on the checklist she prepared for the Butler Institute of American Art's exhibition, while two impressions of the print in the ARTneo collection are titled in graphite *Berenice*.

accessories are not. Sloane experimented with the application of collaged mylar cut-outs to create a dazzling effect in Kent's earring and ring. All of Sloane's portraits of Kent enlist a sense of glamour that engages a Pop perspective, even when they show a more personal and subdued side of the sitter [fig. 5]. By selecting such an extravagant sitter, Sloane contributed to enhancement of a Cleveland icon, a persona who was cherished by many and whose antics and carefree attitude remain a topic of conversation with those who knew her.

With Marjorie Talalay's portrait [fig. 6], Sloane also experiments with technique. As in other prints, she makes use of mylar collage. The black background is screenprinted, while she adds the figure in with acrylic paint. Talalay, along with Nina Sundell, started the New Gallery of Contemporary Art in Cleveland in 1968. There had previously been no venue that was dedicated to exhibiting the changes in art, or work out of New York City. When Sundell left with her husband for Washington D.C., in 1972, Talalay continued the work of maintaining high standards and exhibiting both internationally recognized artists, as well as contemporary artists in the Cleveland region. Her vision led to a broader educational outreach in the community and a shift to a non-profit as the Cleveland Center for

Contemporary Art, which eventually paved the way for the organization to become the Museum of Contemporary Art Cleveland. When the move was made to the Cleveland Playhouse complex in 1990, Sundell returned to Cleveland for the grand opening. She applauded Talalay saying, "This is an extraordinary achievement. Marjorie has always been very generous about the small share I had in getting this started. This is her achievement and she is being very modest." At this point, Talalay broke in and stated, "None of this would have been possible without Nina's vision."[11]

Sloane's use of black as the background color and that of Talalay's clothing suggests to the viewer qualities of both strength and modesty. Talalay's figure is allowed to become one with the background as if to emphasize her willingness to forgo praises of her own achievements in order to let others succeed. Concurrently, black is a color of power. It is elegant and glamorous. Talalay's pose is one of confidence, and black accentuates that. Black is also symbolic of modernity. It is suitable that a champion of contemporary art should be shrouded in the color that is the essence of high fashion in the twentieth century, as well as a conceptual color in the avant-garde: from Suprematism and Constructivism to Abstract Expressionism and Minimalism.

Sloane also used the image of the figure to deconstruct identity. Thus is the case with two portraits of Eugenia Thornton. The first portrait is a large acrylic painting on canvas [fig. 7]. Thornton is seen seated in front

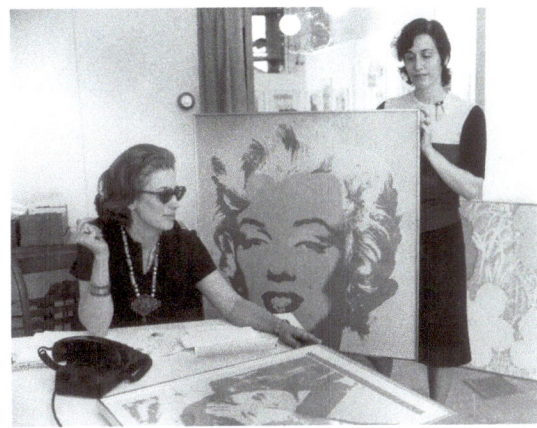

Marjorie Talalay and Nina Sundell (standing) with Warhol's Marilyn, 1969, Courtesy of MOCA Cleveland

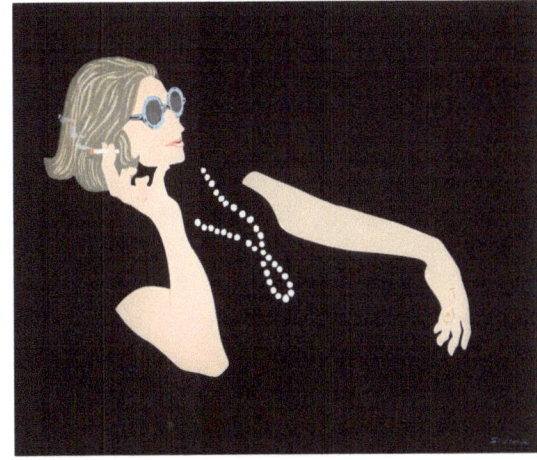

Fig. 6:. *Marjorie Talalay*, 1972, acrylic and screenprint on paper with mylar collage, 15.5 x 20 in., ARTneo Collection, Gift of the artist, 2002-727

11. Mary Strassmeyer, "Art hall opening stops traffic," *The Plain Dealer*, February 11, 1990, 3-G

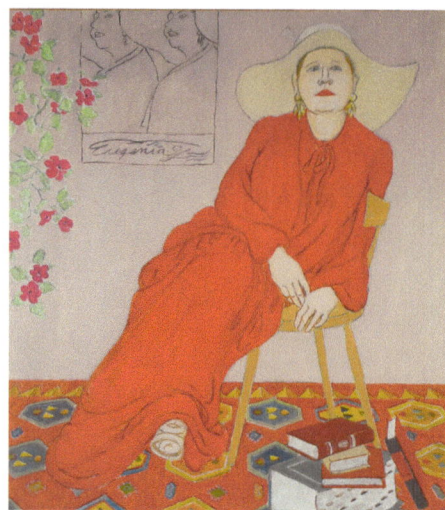

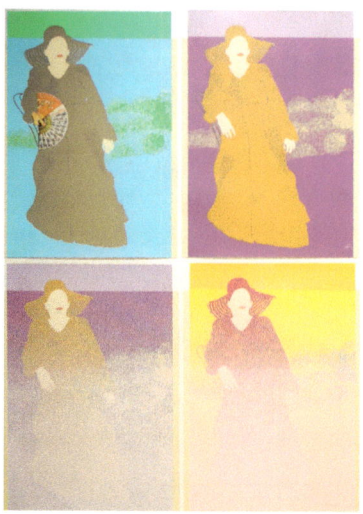

Fig 7. *Eugenia Thornton*, c. 1970, acrylic on paper, 48 x 42 in. ARTneo Collection, Gift of the artist, 2002-720

Fig 8. *Eugenia Thornton*, c. 1970, screenprint on paper, 28 x 20.5 in. ARTneo Collection, Gift of the artist, 2002-720

of a poster with her likeness reproduced twice, her name scrawled across the bottom. The poster is treated in line only, suggesting that her public identity is secondary to her passion. Thornton was a well known bibliophile who wrote many book reviews for *The Plain Dealer* and gave lectures on literature. The stack of books resting in the lower right of the image alludes to her passionate engagement with literature.

As well known as Thornton may have been, the second portrait of her completely conceals her identity [fig. 8]. The four-panel screenprint reduces Thornton's features and removes the books alltogether. Sloane utilizes the Pop terminology of Ben-Day dots that reference the four-color printing process of comic books and newspapers. They first came to prominence in Pop Art with the works of Roy Lichtenstein who created large scale reproductions of print ads and comic book panels that were often manipulated to bridge high and low art. Here, the Ben-Day dots are used more closely with their traditional purpose of changing tonal areas and shading. Through the four panels, the dots help define the shape of the figure. In the lower two panels they begin to obscure the figure, creating a hazy affect that blocks the hard-edged contours of Thornton's body.

Thornton's facial features have been completely removed except for her bright red lips. There is no way of recognizing her identity aside from her name in the title. At this point she becomes anonymous, the repetition of her image further degrading her individuality. Similar to the portraiture of Allan D'Arcangelo, Sloane's use of the faceless female figure to bring up questions of the treatment of women in society and their changing role in a male dominated work environment.

Other works of Sloane's trend towards caricature, with the emphasis in these screenprints being the look of a hand-drawn image. Stylistically, caricature embraces linear qualities with attention to graphic details. A strong mode of abstraction links it back to modern art. Its formulaic approach to depicting recognizable figures relies heavily on a person's essential features, especially those unique to the individual. The exaggeration of the person's appearance creates a quickly identifiable rendering, though, through a false graphic description. E. H. Grombrich states that "All discoveries are discoveries not of likenesses but of equivalences which enable us to see reality in terms of an image and an image in terms of reality...These identities do not depend on the imitation of individual features so much as on the configuration of clues."[12] Through clues, caricatures set out to be a less realistic representation of a person. They are purposefully distorted in such a way that they lead the viewer to a new approach of seeing the identity of the person the work depicts.

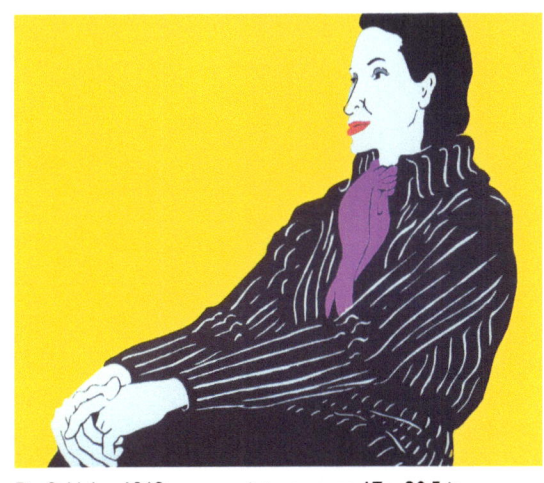

Early in its history, caricature was seen as narrowing the gap between art and life, and had established itself as a comment on current events in eighteenth-century England. The images were mass-produced in print, making periodicals such as *Vanity Fair* the perfect medium for their delivery to the public. The focus on everyday life, current events, and popular culture that caricature expressed along with its broad reach through mass reproduction created proto-Pop imagery.

Helen Borsick wrote of Sloane's work that she "...painted in quick strokes of watercolor or ink brush, elegant without flattery or prettiness, and sometimes leaning to caricature in the simplification."[13] These marks often translated into her prints, including the portrait of Helen Weinberg. *Helen* [fig. 9] is loose in its linear qualities giving the impression of having been drawn or painted by hand. The pose is one of a distinguished and confident woman and the facial features are exaggerated so that her identity can be determined by those familiar with either the sitter, or other images of her. Weinberg had been a professor of literature, composition, and art criticism at the Cleveland Institute of Art. She wrote literary reviews for *The Plain Dealer* and researched and published writings on Cleveland's art history. Weinberg had also been an active art collector, supporting both emerging and established local artists. Her contributions on perceptual art for the exhibition catalogs and self-published magazines of the Anomina Group in the 1960s helped to define the conceptual aspects of the group's work. The bold orange color and linear aspects of Weinberg's blouse allude to her interest in Op Art and geometric abstraction as they define the figural form that otherwise is nondescript.

When creating portraits of artists Paul B. Travis and Edris Eckhardt, Sloane began to further emphasize the recognition of the figures through symbolically exaggerated features much in the style of caricature. The portrait titled *Paul Travis* was based on sketches that were completed during one of Sloane's group life drawing sessions. A student at the Cleveland School of Art in 1913, Travis returned after serving in the military during World War I in 1920 to teach at the school for the next 37 years. Many of the members in the life drawing group had previously been his students. They had approached Travis to sit for them, and he graciously agreed to pose for the artists and arrived wearing a yellow plaid shirt with a brightly colored print tie. Sloane was one of the first to produce a finished work from the day of sketching with a screenprint aptly titled, *Paul Travis* [fig. 10] in 1970. The image depicts Travis in profile using a two-screen pattern of yellow ochre and black on white paper. The colors, remarked Helen Borsick, "are tiger colors, and how appropriate for the portrait of a man who's known far and wide for his paintings of tigers and jungle scenes."[14]

12. E. H. Grombrich, *Art and Illusion* (Princeton: Princeton University Press, 1969), 345.
13. Helen Borsick, "Toward Togetherness with Science," *The Plain Dealer*, November 2, 1969, 4-G.
14. Helen Borsick, "How to Capture a Master," *The Plain Dealer*, February 22, 1970, 10-F.

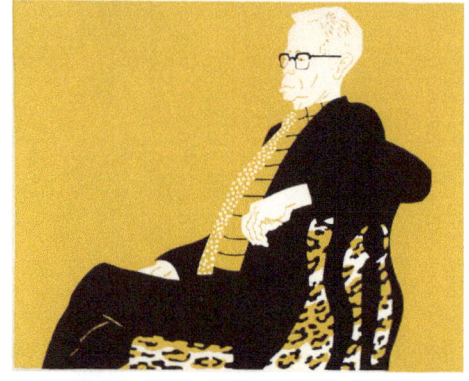

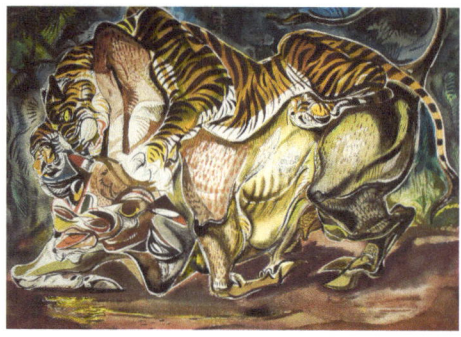

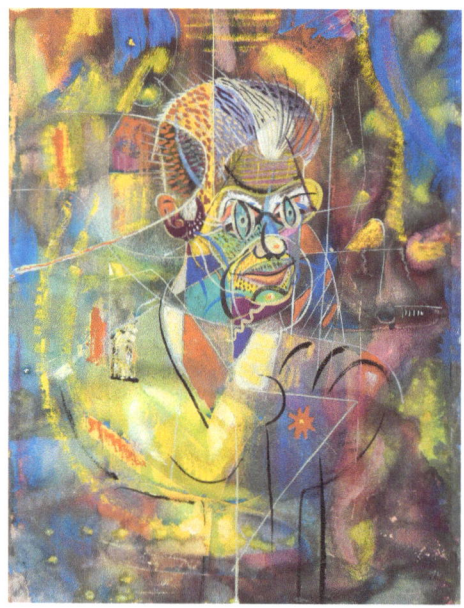

Fig 10. *Paul Travis*, 1970, screenprint on paper, 17 x 20.5 in. ARTneo Collection, 1986-145

Fig 11. Paul Travis, *Tiger and Bullock*, 1951, watercolor on paper, 28.5 x 36.5 in. ARTneo Collection, 1994-349

Fig 12. Paul Travis, *Self Portrait*, 1956, watercolor and gouache on paper, 26 x 19.5 in. ARTneo Collection, 2002-704

Travis is then seen in the light of his own artwork. Patterns on the tie and in the fabric of the chair paired with color are the clues to his identity along with the exaggerated facial features of his forehead and jaw line. However, stress is placed not on his personal features, but those elements that link him to his paintings of tigers and African scenes. To Travis, Africa was an answer to the problem of Europe having been previously exhausted of inspiration by generations of other artists.[15] Through the elements in the print that recall African motifs, his identity becomes tied to his work.[16] Using caricature, Sloane reminds the viewer of Travis's vast oeuvre and his yearning to create works of art inspired by places untouched by western civilization.

Less exaggerated in appearance but still using the techniques of caricature, Sloane's portrait of sculptor Edris Eckhardt[17] [fig. 13] is transformed through three different works. Based on a life drawing originally executed in watercolor, Sloane created two prints of the artist, one screenprint on white paper and another screenprint on handmade paper. Subtle differences can be observed, the first being the texture of the papers. Compositionally, the shape of the handmade paper results in the adjustment of Eckhardt's hand. In both prints, a great deal of attention is paid to the hands. Their placement in the composition emphasizes their importance as an identifier of the sitter. They are the tools with which Eckhardt created her art. Further, the background color brings to mind the color of clay while the symmetrical form created by her arms conjures the silhouette of a ceramic vase. The use of handmade paper further emphasizes the sculptural allusion.

When her reduction of the figure was at it's peak, Sloane produced works like *Mrs. M.* [fig. 14]. The work depicts ceramicist Dorathee Manbeck of whom Sloane created an image of pure design. In the print the background color shifts to the foreground when the yellow pattern of Manbeck's dress surrounds it. Sloane skillfully uses the surface designs found in popular fashion to illustrate the volume of Manbeck's figure in an optical construct based on color theory in *Interaction of Color*. These theories come from color studies of Josef Albers, in which he showed how colors appear to change hue while retraining the same pigment when surrounded by other colors. *Mrs. M.* is not a pure example of this

15. Helen Borsick, "Toward Togetherness with Science," *The Plain Dealer*, November 2, 1969, 4-G.

16. Travis identified himself with the image of the tiger, though there are no tigers in Africa. Their inspiration contained the same exotic and strange qualities that he felt in Africa. He started drawing tigers at the Cleveland Zoo in 1951, and many of the works can be seen as self-portraits [fig. 11]. Travis even created a self-portrait as tiger [fig. 12].
Henry Adams, *Paul Travis: 1891-1975* (Cleveland: Cleveland Artists Foundation, 2002), 49.

17. Like Paul Travis, Edris Eckardt attended and taught at the Cleveland School of Art. She studied there from 1927 to 1931 and began teaching in 1933, continuing through 1961. She also served as the Head of the Sculpture and Ceramics Division, Cleveland District, Works Progress Administration Federal Art Project from 1935 to 1941.

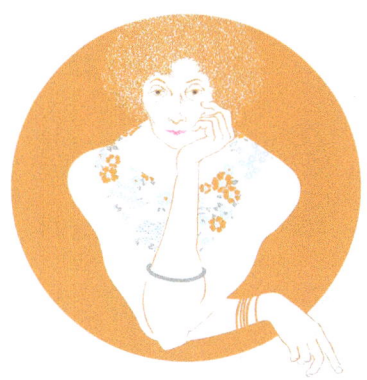

Fig 13. *Edris*, 1976, screenprint on handmade paper, 20 x 19 in. ARTneo Collection, 1998-418

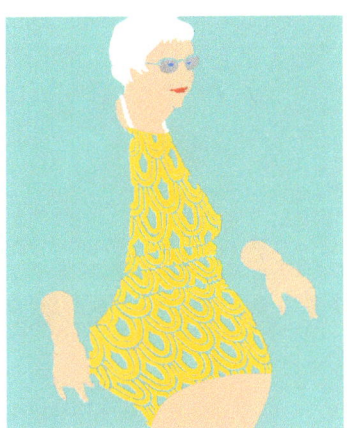

Fig 14. *Mrs. M*, 1969, screenprint on paper with mylar collage, 20.75 x 17 in., ARTneo Collection, Gift of the artist, 2002-247

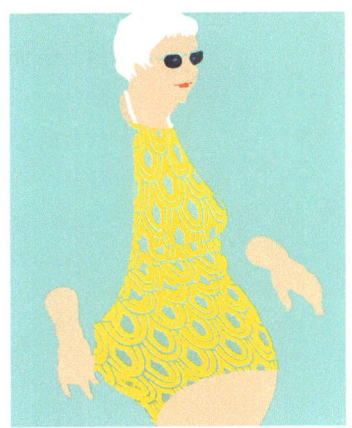

Fig 15. *Mrs. M*, 1969, screenprint on paper with mylar collage, 20.75 x 17 in., ARTneo Collection, Gift of the artist, 2002-802

technique, as another example of this screenprint [fig. 15] paired with the first conflicts with the Pop concept of mass-produced images.

Typically artists strived to achieve uniformity from one impression to the next. Both impressions of *Mrs. M.* should be nearly identical through the rigorous screenprinting process based on proofs to examine the behavior of the ink. It is noticeable that these two images show inaccuracies and differences in the image. The yellow ink is not precisely placed, causing a break in the hard edge forms of the pattern. This is caused by Sloane's watering down of the printing inks. She purposefully diluted ink to allow for inconsistencies from impression to impression in some of her prints. This challenges the notion of mass-produced identical objects that Pop artists generally glorified. On the topic of industrial design Sloane stated "I don't really like mass-produced items even when they are well designed. I like the individual touch and the one of a kind."[18] Sloane also experimented with blotting the ink before it dried to allow the background color to come through to create unique images that are still in essence a multiple.

Sloane's approach to the use of ink shows the dual affect of what constitutes a unique image versus that of an identical one. Her method reflects the examination of struggle with the machine age's homogenization of objects in contemporary culture that Pop Art engaged. It also challenges the concept of what an edition actually is and how it functions as a work of art. Through printmaking, a piece is produced and is typically identical, or as close to being identical as possible. The public as well as dealers and artists view the process as simply multiplying a single image. This has allowed for a more democratic way to collect art by allowing multiples to be sold at a lower price point than that of a unique painting. Prints present a paradox in the concept that the process produces many identical but unique originals.[19] With this in mind, it becomes clear why Pop artists had a fascination with multiples.

For many, the production of editions was not an aesthetic activity. Instead it relied

18. Recorded Interview: Elizabeth McClelland, December 1977, 35:40, Audio File, ARTneo Archival Collection.
19. Timothy Van Laar, "Printmaking: Editions as Artworks," *Journal of Aeshtetic Education*, Vol. 14, No. 4, Special Issue: "The Government, Art, and Aesthetic Education," October, 1980, 98.

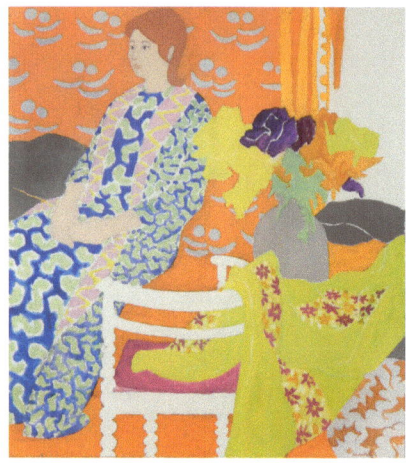

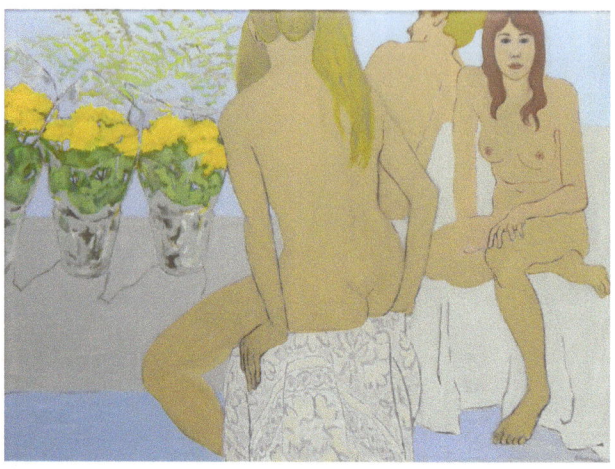

Fig 16. *Woman in Flowered Robe*, 1969,
Acrylic on canvas, 48 x 42 in. Courtesey of
Rachel Davis Fine Arts

Fig 17. *3 Nudes*, 1973, acrylic on canvas, 47 x 68 in. Collection of
Phyllis and Bob Lester

on a market demand and an idea of quantity. The materials and process-oriented
production method are means to an end, but do not give a reason for an artist wanting
to make editions beyond that of accessibility to a wider audience. By watering her inks
Sloane acheived an edition of variations printed from the same screens bu also creates
a disrupted spatial relationship to the edition. With each impression being unique, the
entire edition becomes a singular work of art. The impressions become individual parts
of a whole, which is then broken up and separated by space as the prints are divided and
moved to other locations. This allows for the image to be viewed in many places at the
same time, but the whole effect of the edition is only seen when all of the impressions
are brought together in the same space at the same time.

The use of surface design and pattern becomes the subject of the work in *Woman in
Flowered Robe*. [fig. 16] In this painting, the figure becomes completely integrated into the
background through the flatness of the picture plane and emphasis on pattern, "I get so
involved in some of the design elements that I never really think about the subject matter,
as you say, removed from the ugliness of the world. I certainly don't want them to be
pretty sweet."[20] In this way, the sitter becomes an object within a still-life composition and
is no longer the primary representational goal. The identity isn't even considered; rather
both the image and the title emphasize the concept of pattern and the idea of design.

In *3 Nudes* [fig. 17] Sloane continues the treatment of the figure as an object. The
nudes become a compositional element by repeating the three pots of flowers, creating a balance in the image. The figures, though closely arranged, have an isolation that
detaches them from both one another and the viewer. Even the gaze of the farthest
right figure is off in the distance, not engaging the viewer. The poses, two with their
backs turned to the viewer and one frontal view, are very matter of fact. They deny
the male gaze through the lack of any sexual connotation. This also runs against the
male-driven objectification of women in Pop Art. Artists like Tom Wesselmann created
sexually explicit images, depicting the female figure as an anonymous mass produced
object ready for male consumption. Like Sloane, he drew directly from life. Wesselmann reduced an individual to a sexual object through lack of identifiable and unique
features. While Sloane has a similar effect in her nudes, her works do not display erotic
qualities. She is instead interested in the figure as a non-being, a substitute for a piece

20. Recorded Interview: Elizabeth McClelland, December 1977, 20:23, Audio File, ARTneo Archival Collection.

of furniture or other decorative item with which to break up space.

In her prints of nudes [fig. 18 and fig. 19], the linear quality and choice of color lend a sense of whimsy to the works. The poses and features contrast with that immediate care-free reading with one more somber, or melancholy. It is unclear if Sloane meant this to be a statement on the sexist attitudes of contemporary society in the 1960s and 1970s, but she did acknowledge that women as subject did have a connection to feminism and the Women's Liberation Movement, "We had these sketch groups. We always had women models because the men were always working."[21] She did not set out to explore the beauty of women, but through her choices of sitters and how they were portrayed she made a statement on gender roles in society with her choice of subjects.

Helen Weinberg wrote that "...there is constant evidence that more women are seeing the world through a feminist lens."[22] Within Pop Art, women artists were relatively absent from the recognized leaders of the movement. Many dealing with Pop, like Pauline Boty and Rosalyn Drexler, worked on the boundaries, and instead focused on proto-feminist ideas by establishing the female gaze to subvert the objectification of women and turn it instead upon men. Kalliopi Minioudaki writes of Pop Art and women artists that she has "learnt to distrust the canon for its unshakable masculinist foundations..."[23] Yet she defends their dialogue with Pop, adding that the female perspective expands the scope of Pop's socio-political examinations.

Sloane also struggled with the role in which the domestic woman found herself in a changing society. She had left her job at PDA upon the birth of her first child. While she began to dislike industrial design, having a newborn and raising a family did play a role in the decision. In the 1970s, women began to see themselves as in a struggle with the position of men in the workplace. The conflict between a career and the "institutionalized

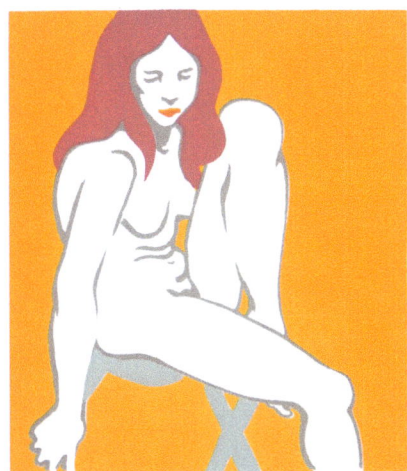

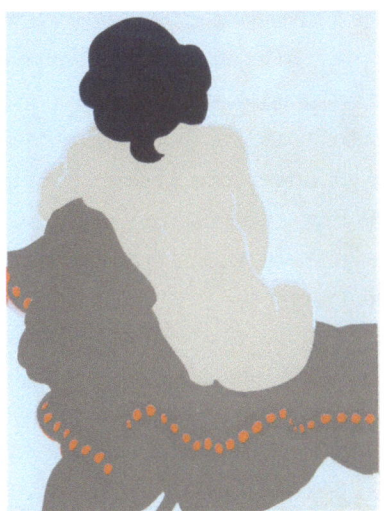

Fig 18. *Untitled* [Nude], 1973, screenprint on paper, 7 x 6 in. ARTneo Collection, Gift of the artist, 2002-771

Fig 19. *Untitled* [Nude], 1973, screenprint on paper, 8 x 6 in. ARTneo Collection, Gift of the artist, 2002-772

21. Peterson, "No Sloane Down."
22. Helen Weinberg, "More She, Less He," *The Plain Dealer*, August 16, 1970, 7-F.
23. Kalliopi Minioudaki, "Pop's Ladies and Bad Girls: Axell, Pauline Boty and Rosalyn Drexler," *Oxford Art Journal*, March 30, 2007, 406.
24. Sylvia Clavan, "Women's Liberation and the Family," *The Family Coordinator*, Vol. 19, No. 4, October, 1970, 321.

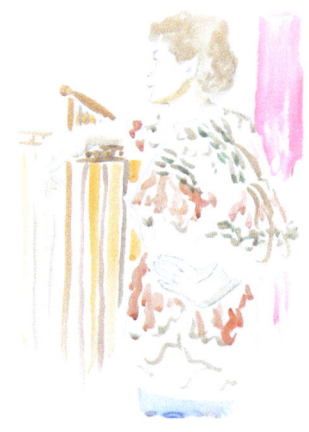

Fig 20. *Elaine Cohen*, 1969, watercolor and graphite on paper, 23 x 17 in. ARTneo Collection, Gift of the artist, 2002-808

normative expectations of the female in American society...," where she was required to "...regard her wife-mother-homemaker role as primary,"[24] became a leading concern of the Women's Liberation movement. Berenice Kent commented that, "Most of the women I've met are so dull, so limited in their lives between grocery lists, picking up children, and housecleaning."[25]

This is not the case with Sloane. While she did leave her job in 1949 to start a family, she was then free to begin making fine and decorative art in the media of ceramics, enamels, paintings, and prints. Speaking about how being an artist affected her role in the family, Sloane said:

> At different points in my life, it was very much a problem and I've seen it in other younger women artists who have small children. I used to feel guilty all the time because I never stopped working. I would always be very anxious when the kids were little to get them to nap so I could run to the studio and start doing some work. And also the guilt about things you should be doing about the house. I sorta had the feeling for a number of years that no matter what I was doing, I should be doing something else.[26]

Though she may have struggled, Sloane managed to include her children in the work she created. This bridged the gap between her two roles as an artist and as a mother.

The women in Sloane's portraits worked to change the status of women in society. To some women like Elaine Cohen [fig. 20], work came more naturally. Of her success in furniture design, Elaine Cohen stated, "I never had the feeling I was having a career. I wasn't programmed to want a career."[27] For Cohen, the projects seemed to evolve from one to another. Many of the women in Sloane's portraits had strong leading roles in their fields. Her depictions of these figures in the language of Pop Art created a narrative of the energy found in Cleveland in those years surrounding the arts.

Sloane's continuous experimentation with creative methods and new materials paired with her design approach to composition parallels the fundamentals of Pop Art. Her choice of subjects and her renderings of them create iconic images that are not only symbols of her sitters, but also symbolic of the time in Cleveland in which they were created. As Pop Art developed through the 1960s and 1970s from imagery based on consumerism to more social and political issues, Sloane's work kept in step with the conceptual shifts. In some ways, how Sloane treated the figure even preceded aspects of Pop's evolution. To say that Phyllis Sloane is a Pop artist would be inaccurate. However, the influences are visible and valuable in the examination of her own artistic growth. With a vast and broad career in fine art, Sloane's body of work allows for new interpretations. Pop became a cultural phenomenon, its reach was vast and Sloane skillfully applied its language to her works, emphasizing her interest in the figure through its means.

25. "Berenice Kent," *The Plain Dealer, Sunday Plain Dealer Magazine*, 12 (ARTneo Clipping File, "Phyllis Sloane").
26. Recorded Interview: Elizabeth McClelland, December 1977, 50:27, Audio File, ARTneo Archival Collection.
27. Barbara Mayer, "Women are finding more jobs in furniture industry," *The Plain Dealer*, October 8, 1983, 14-E.

Plates

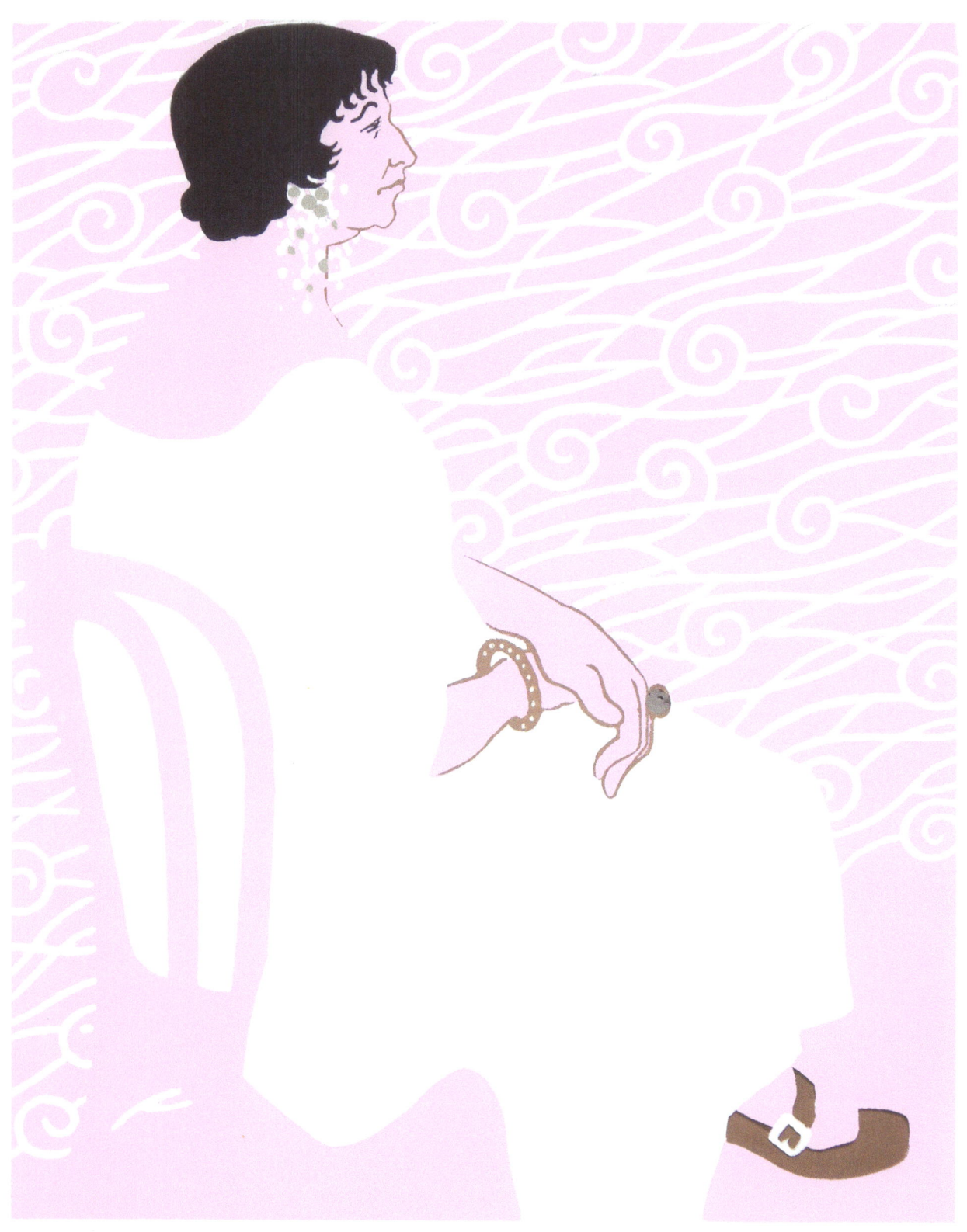

Berenice, 1969
Screenprint and mylar on paper, 22.75 x 18 in.
ARTneo Collection, 1986-283

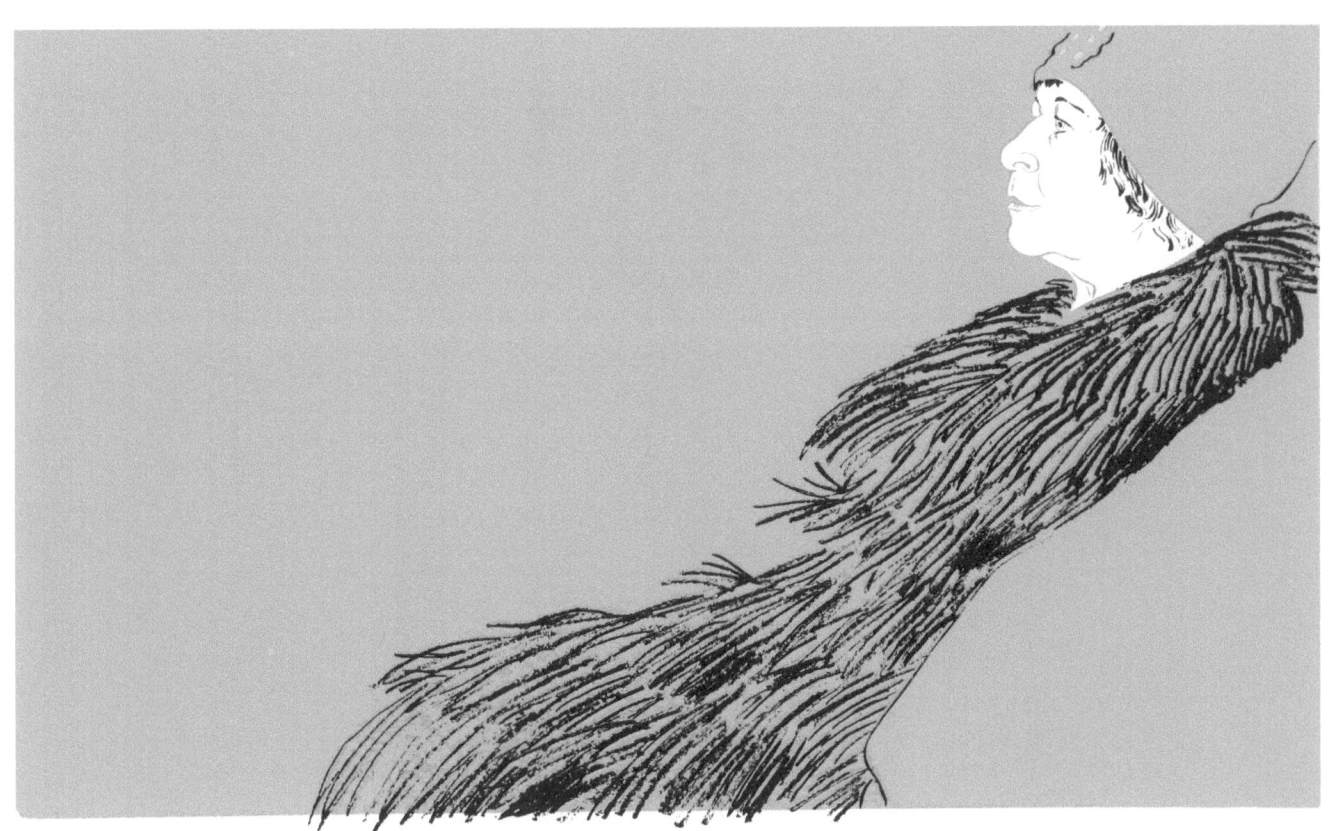

Berenice, 1969
Screenprint on paper, 11 x 18 in.
ARTneo Collection, 1986-254

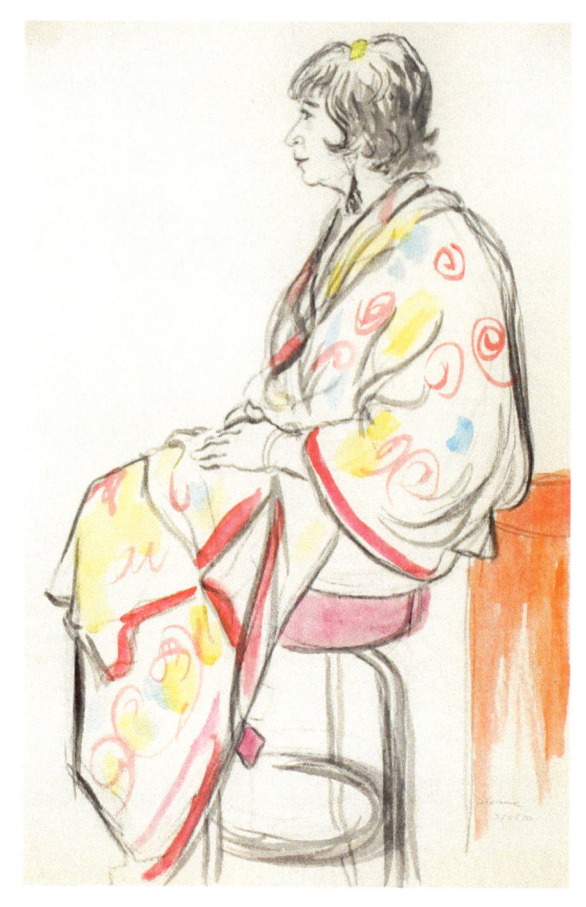

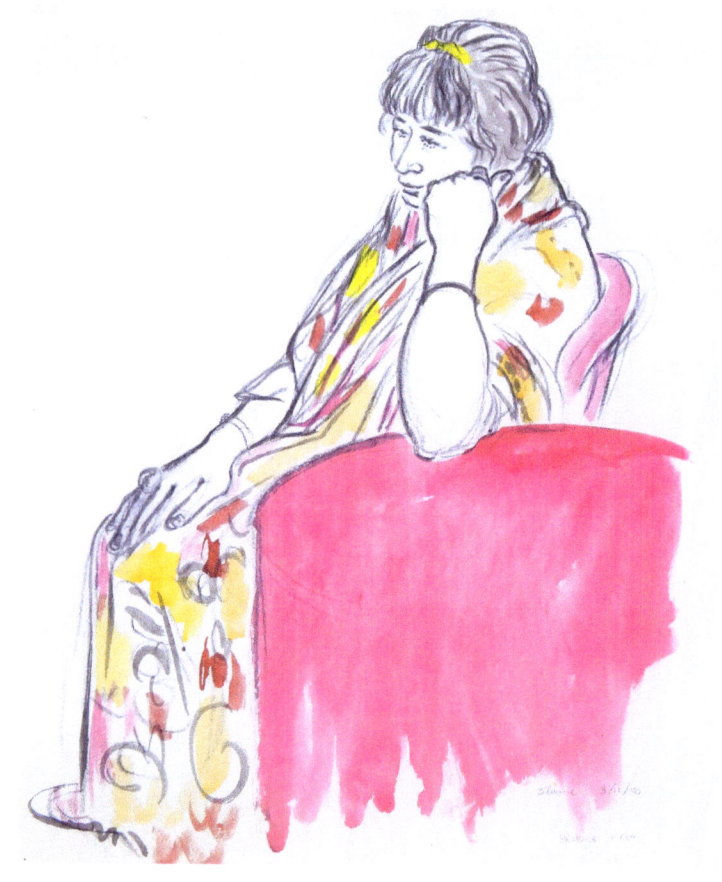

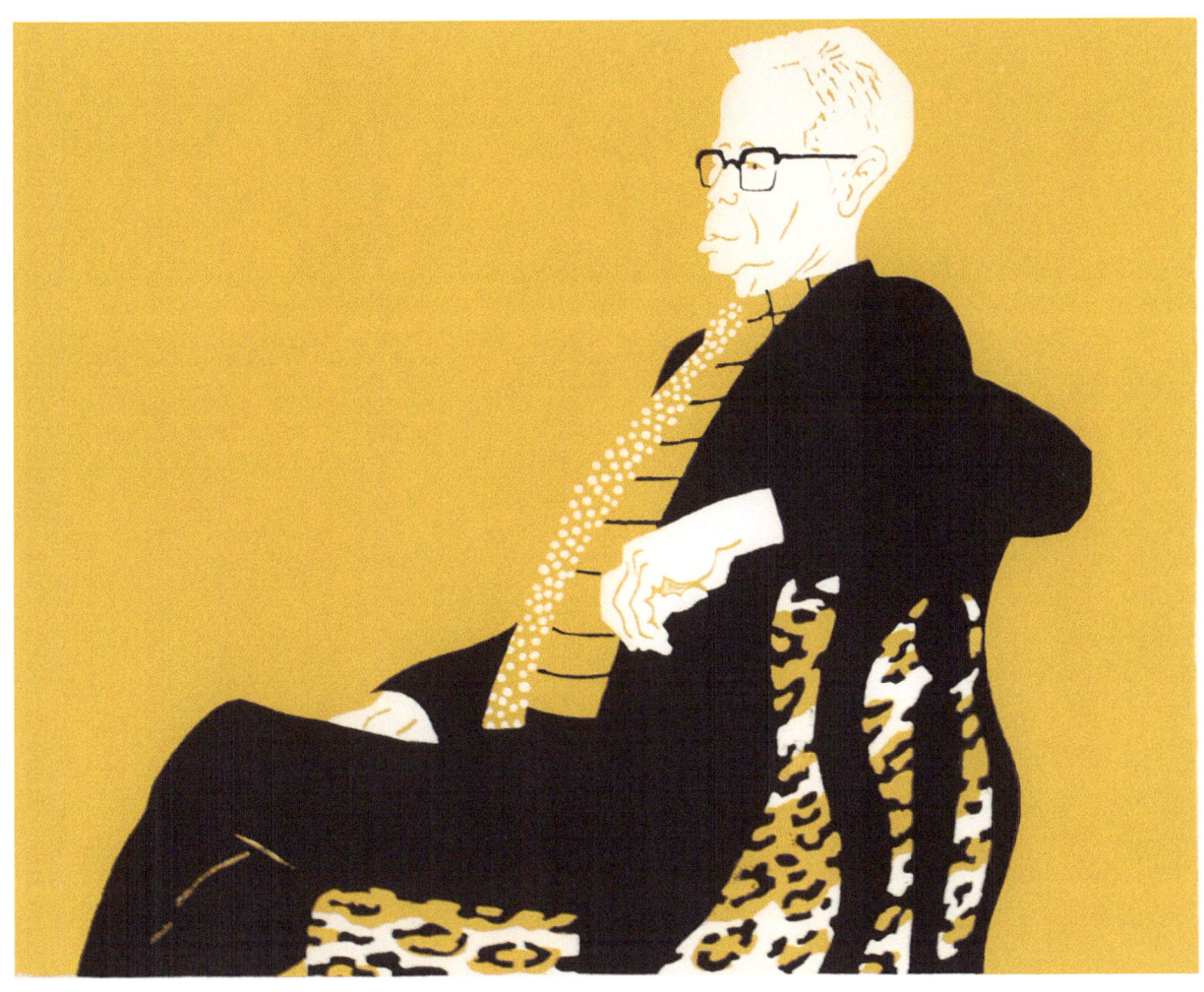

Paul Travis, 1970
Screenprint on paper, 17 x 20.5 in.
ARTneo Collection, 1986-145

Opposite page
Berenice Kent, 1970
Charcoal and watercolor on paper, 24 x 16 in.
ARTneo Collection, Gift of the artist, 2002-247

Berenice Kent, 1970
Charcoal and watercolor on paper, 25 x 20 in.
ARTneo Collection, Gift of the artist, 2002-809

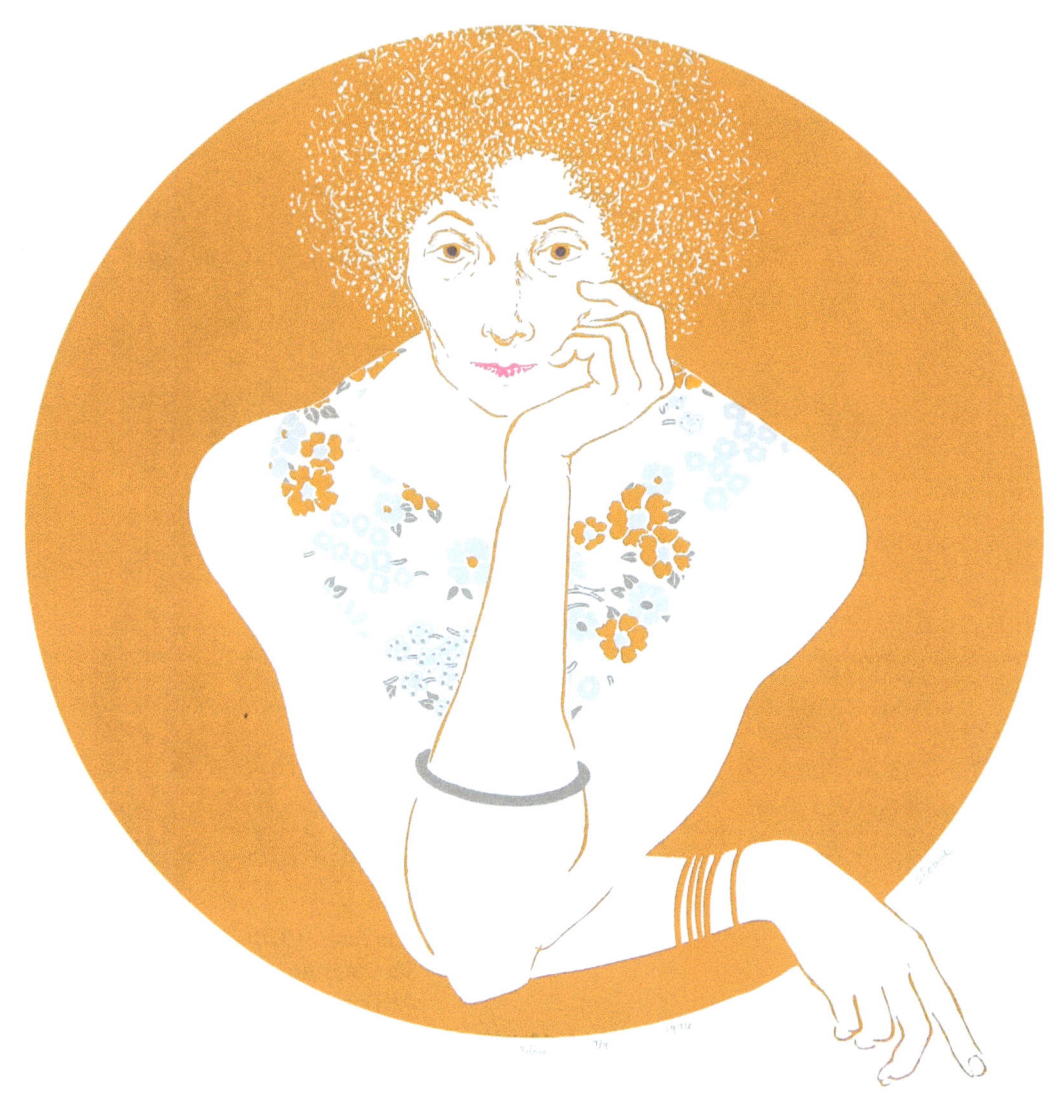

Edris, 1976
Screenprint on paper, 20 x 19 in.
ARTneo Collection, Gift of the artist, 2002-788

Opposite page
Edris, 1976
Screenprint on handmade paper, 20 x 19 in.
ARTneo Collection, 1998-418

Untitled (Edris Eckhardt), 1976
Watercolor and graphite on paper, 14 x 10.5 in.
ARTneo Collection, 1998-417

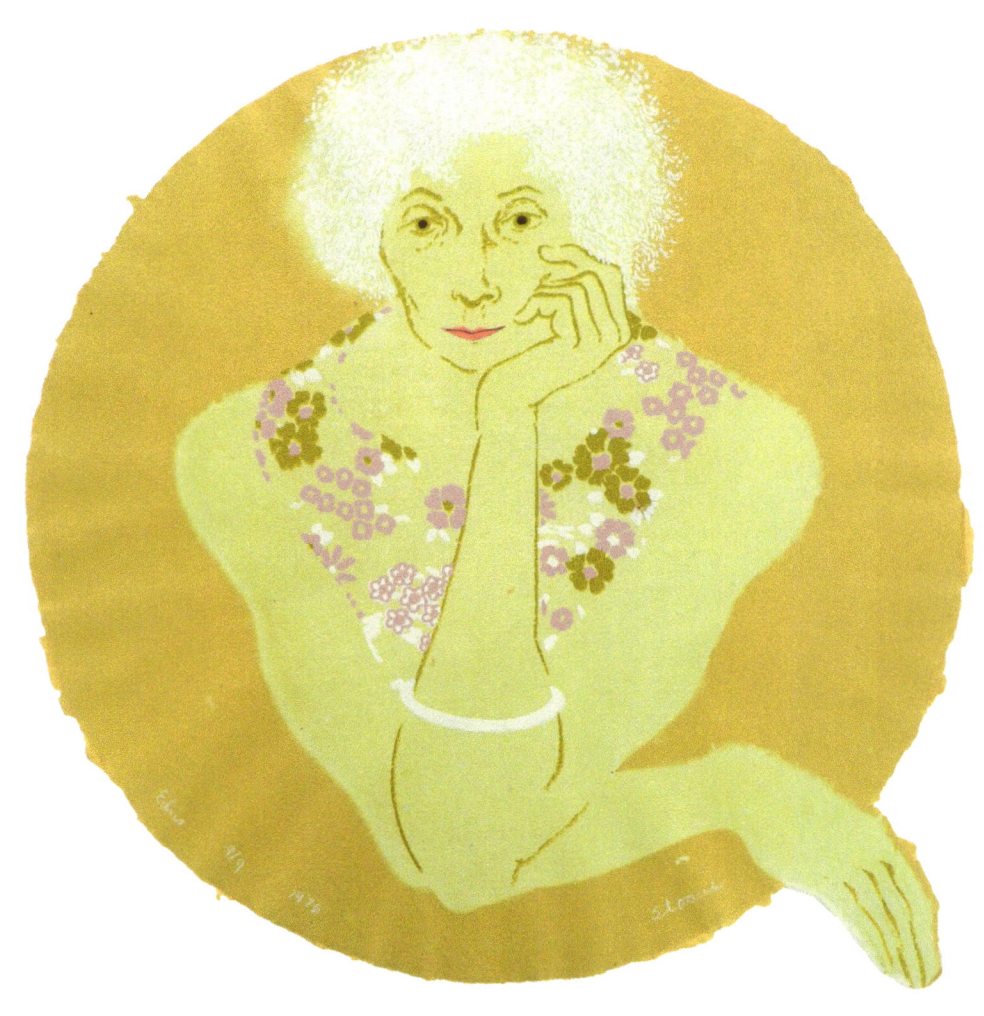

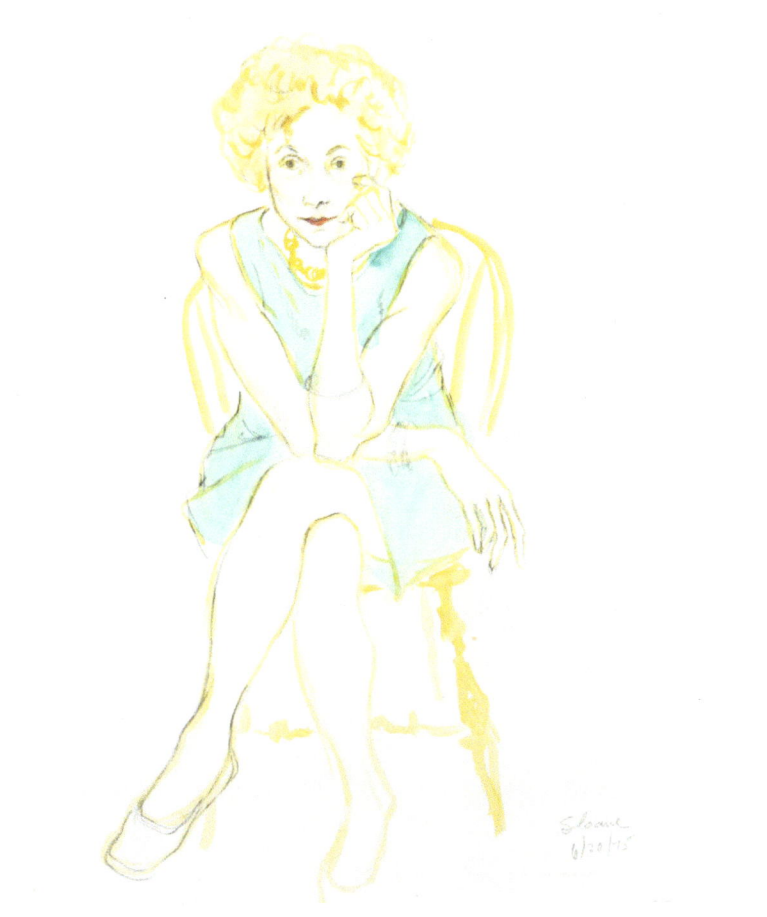

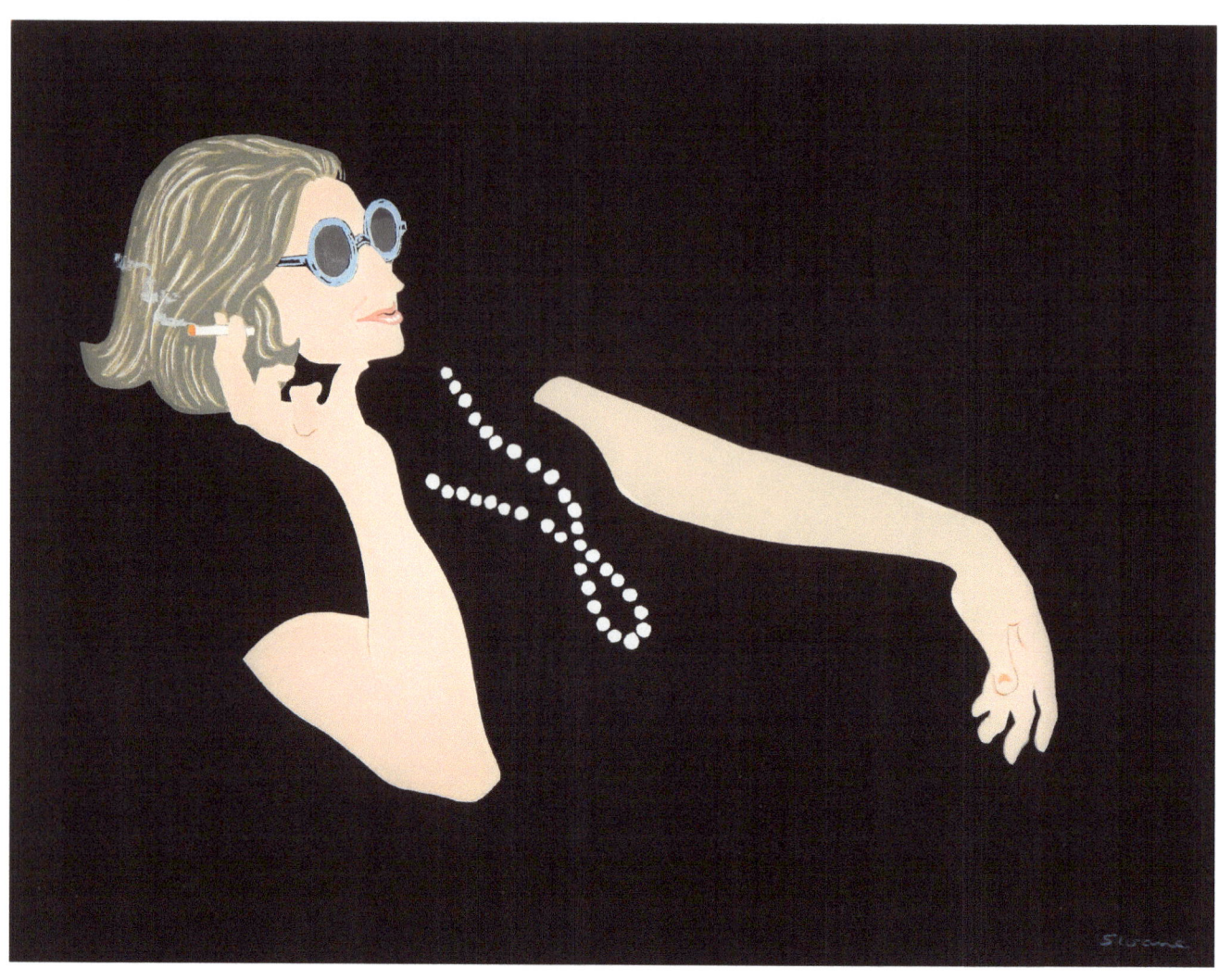

Marjorie Talalay, 1972
Acrylic and screenprint on paper with mylar collage, 15.5 x 20 in.
ARTneo Collection, Gift of the artist, 2002-727

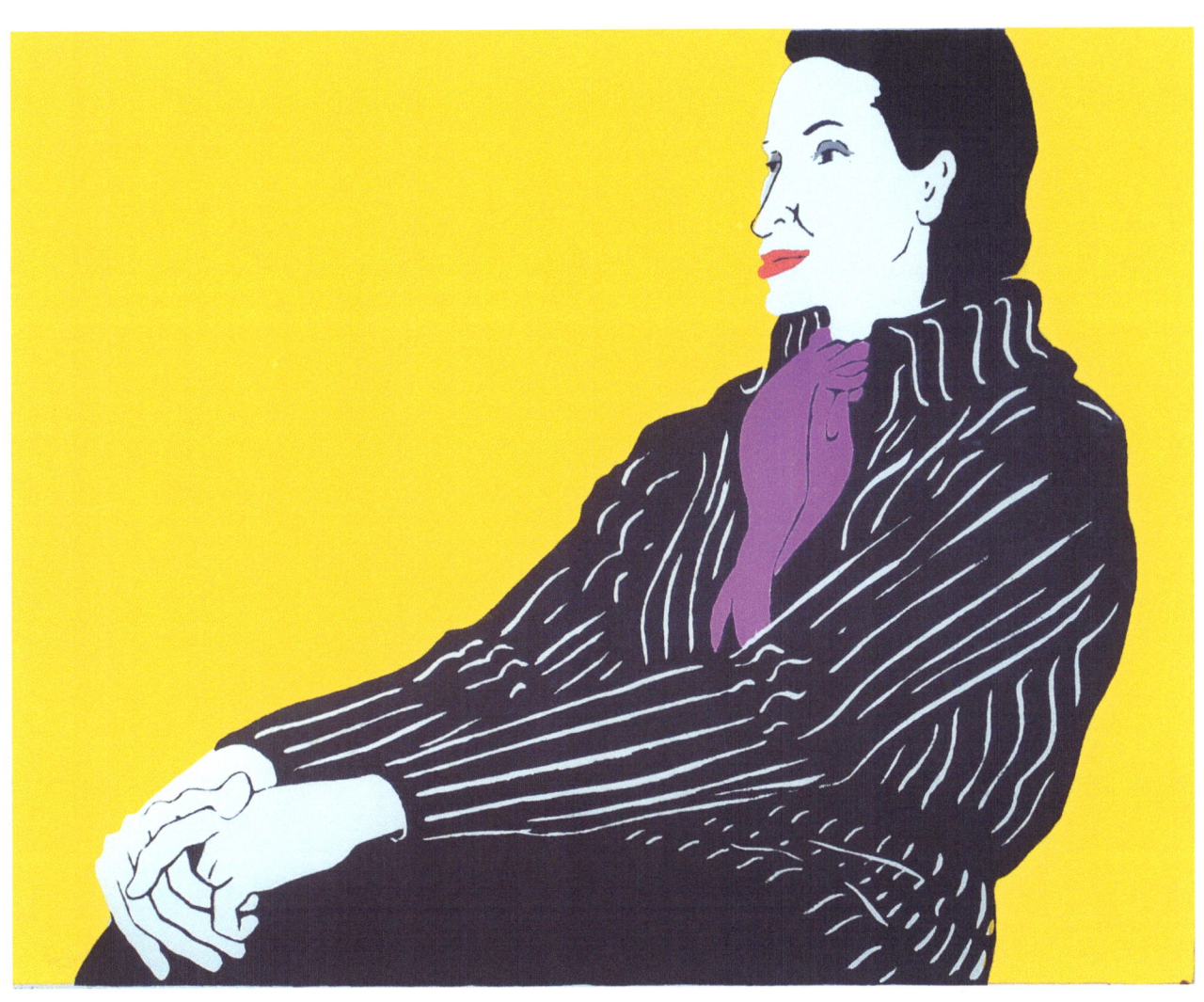

Helen, 1969
Screenprint on paper, 17 x 20.5 in.
ARTneo Collection, Gift of the artist, 2002-726

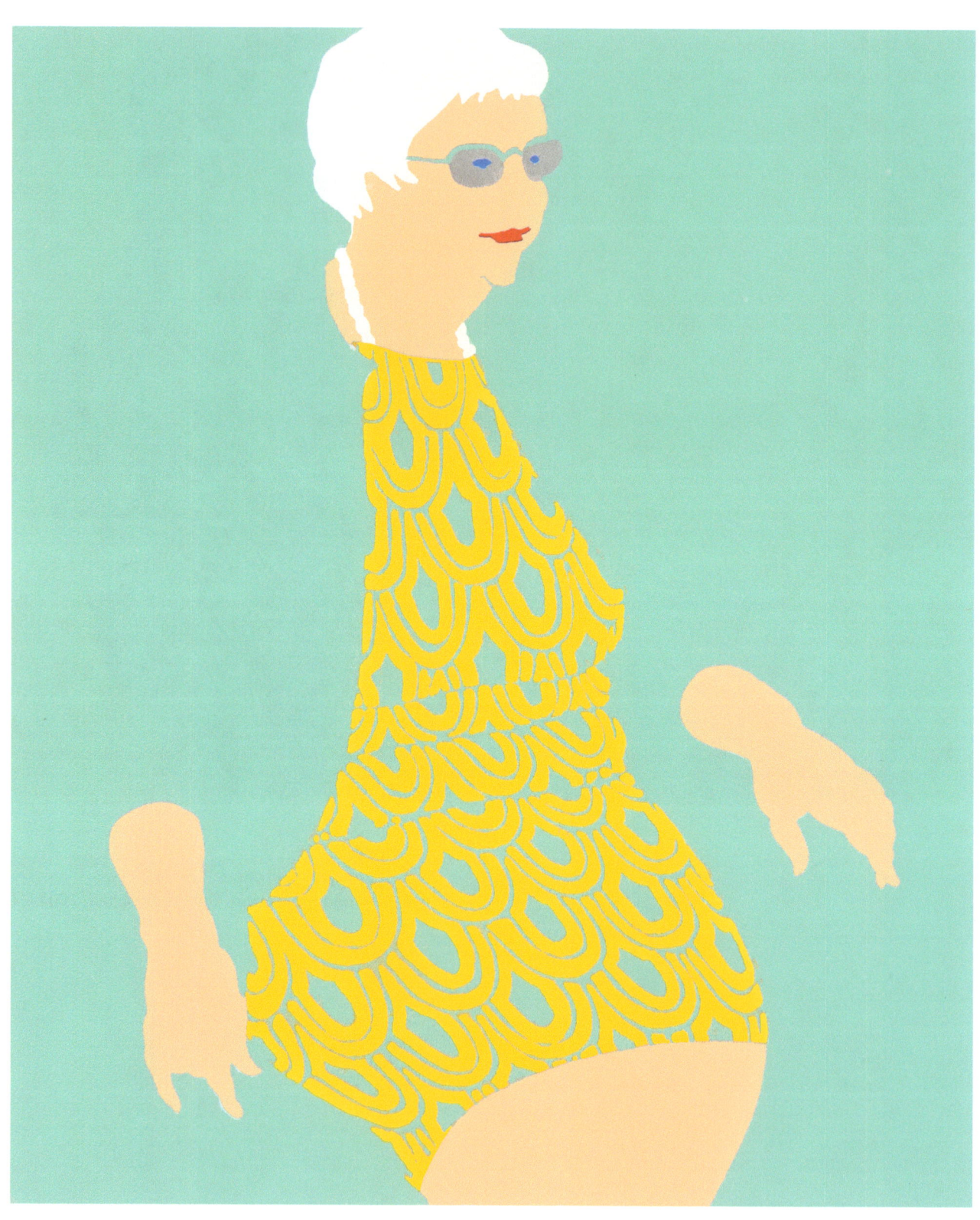

Mrs. M., 1969
Screenprint on paper with mylar collage, 20.75 x 17 in.
ARTneo Collection, Gift of the artist, 2002-147

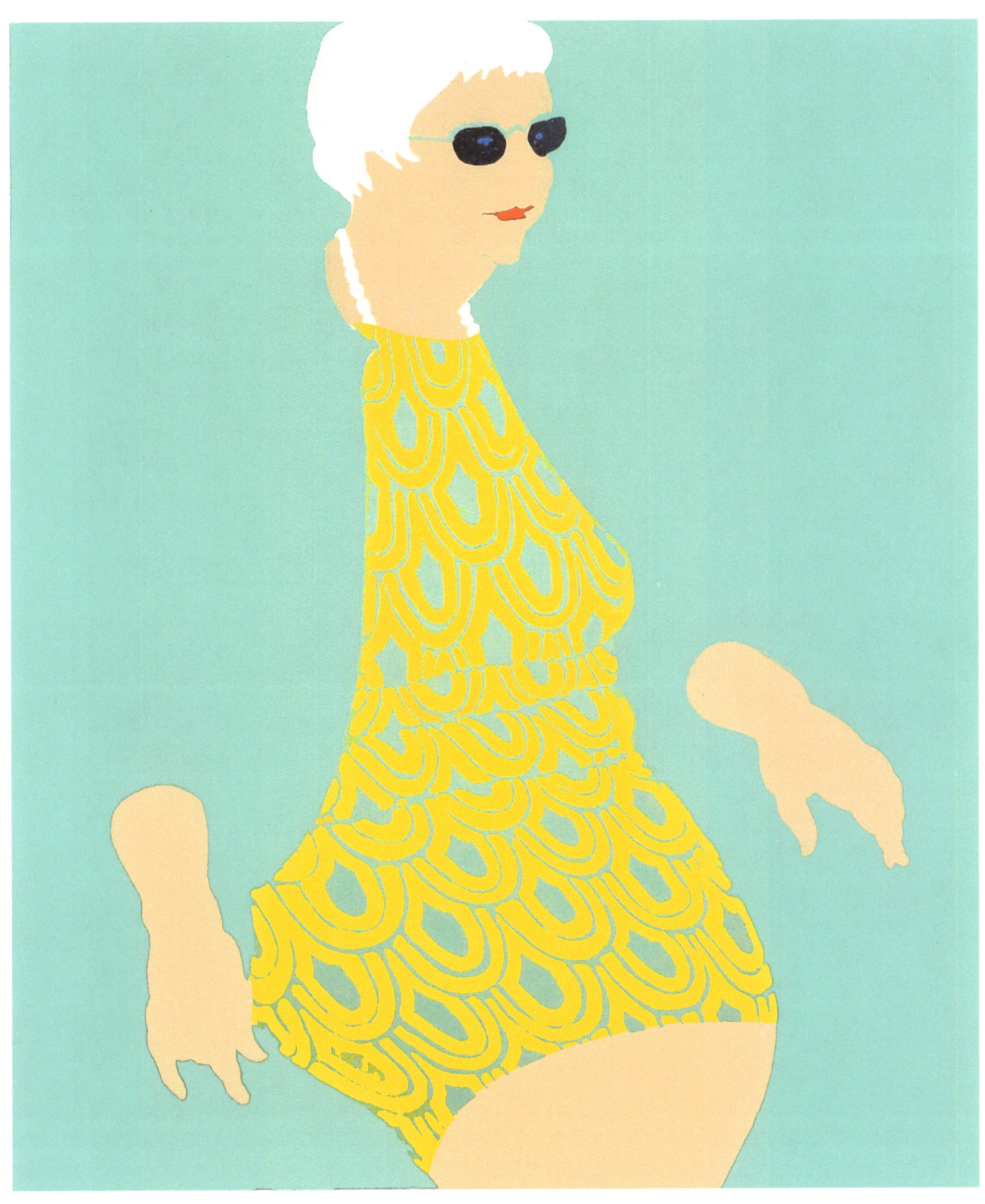

Mrs. M., 1969
Screenprint on paper with mylar collage, 20.75 x 17 in.
ARTneo Collection, Gift of the artist, 2002-802

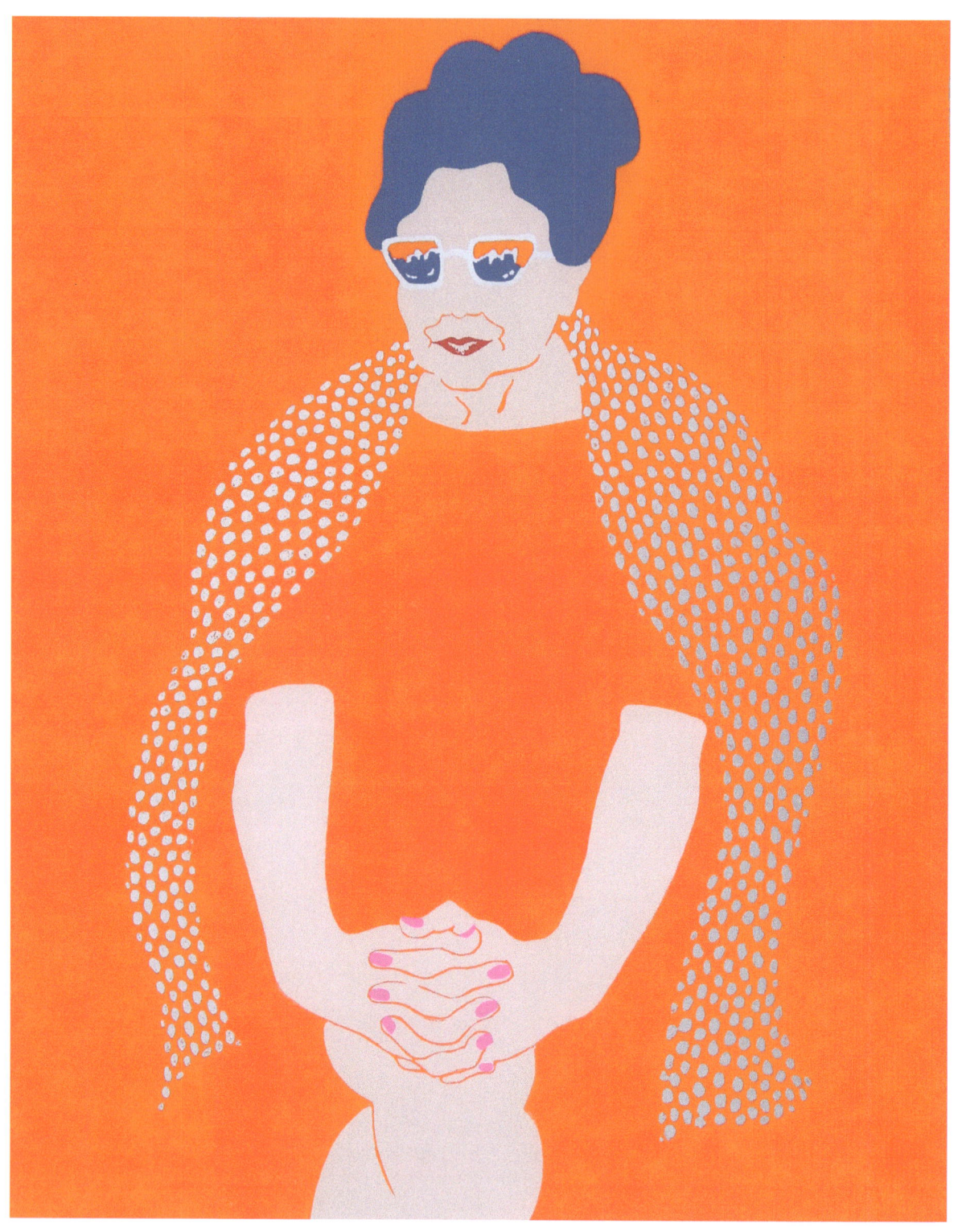

Rose, 1970
Screenprint on silver posterboard, 22.5 x 18.5 in.
ARTneo Collection, Gift of the artist, 2002-815

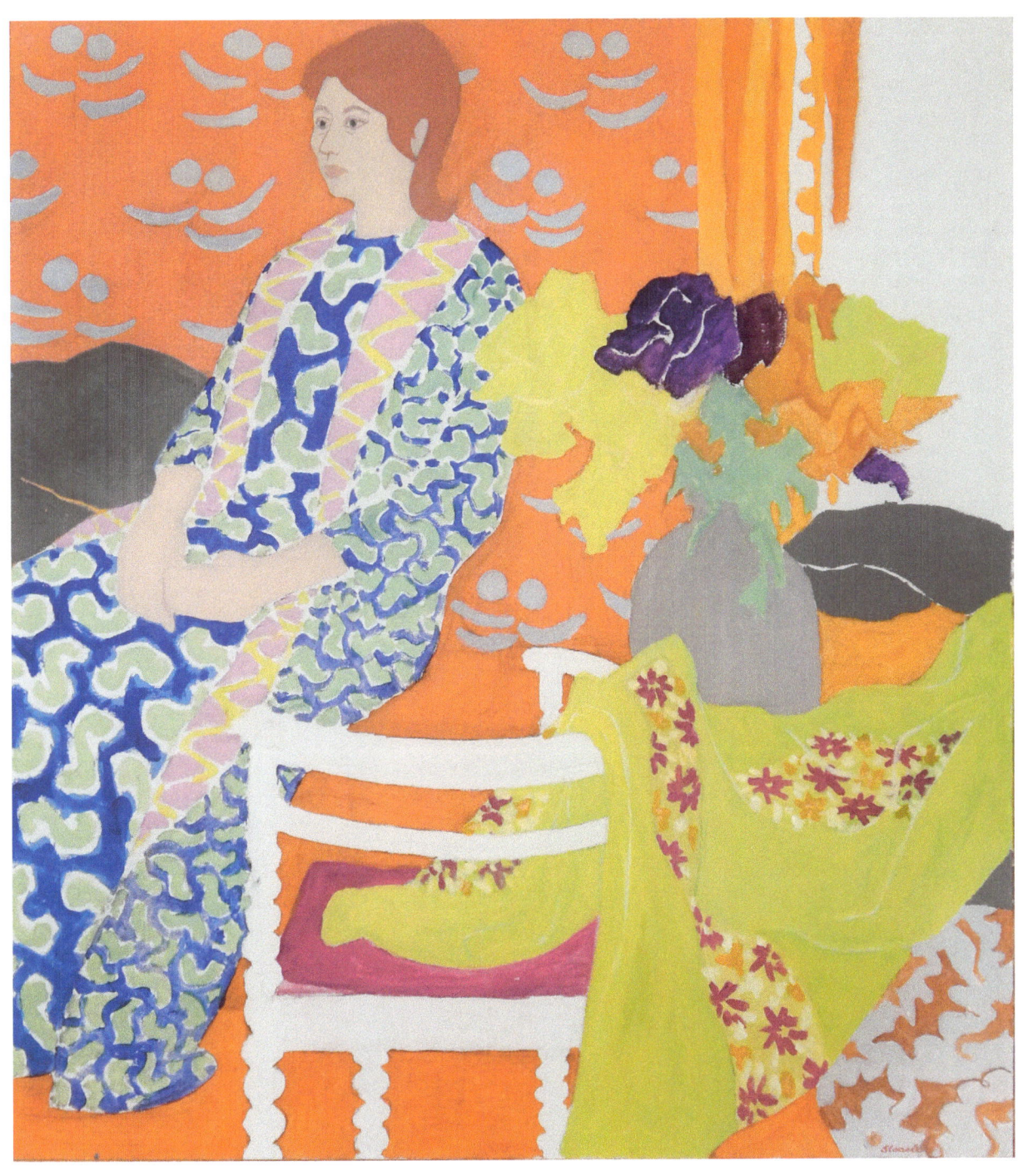

Woman in Flowered Robe, 1969
Acrylic on canvas, 48 x 42 in.
Courtesey of Rachel Davis Fine Arts

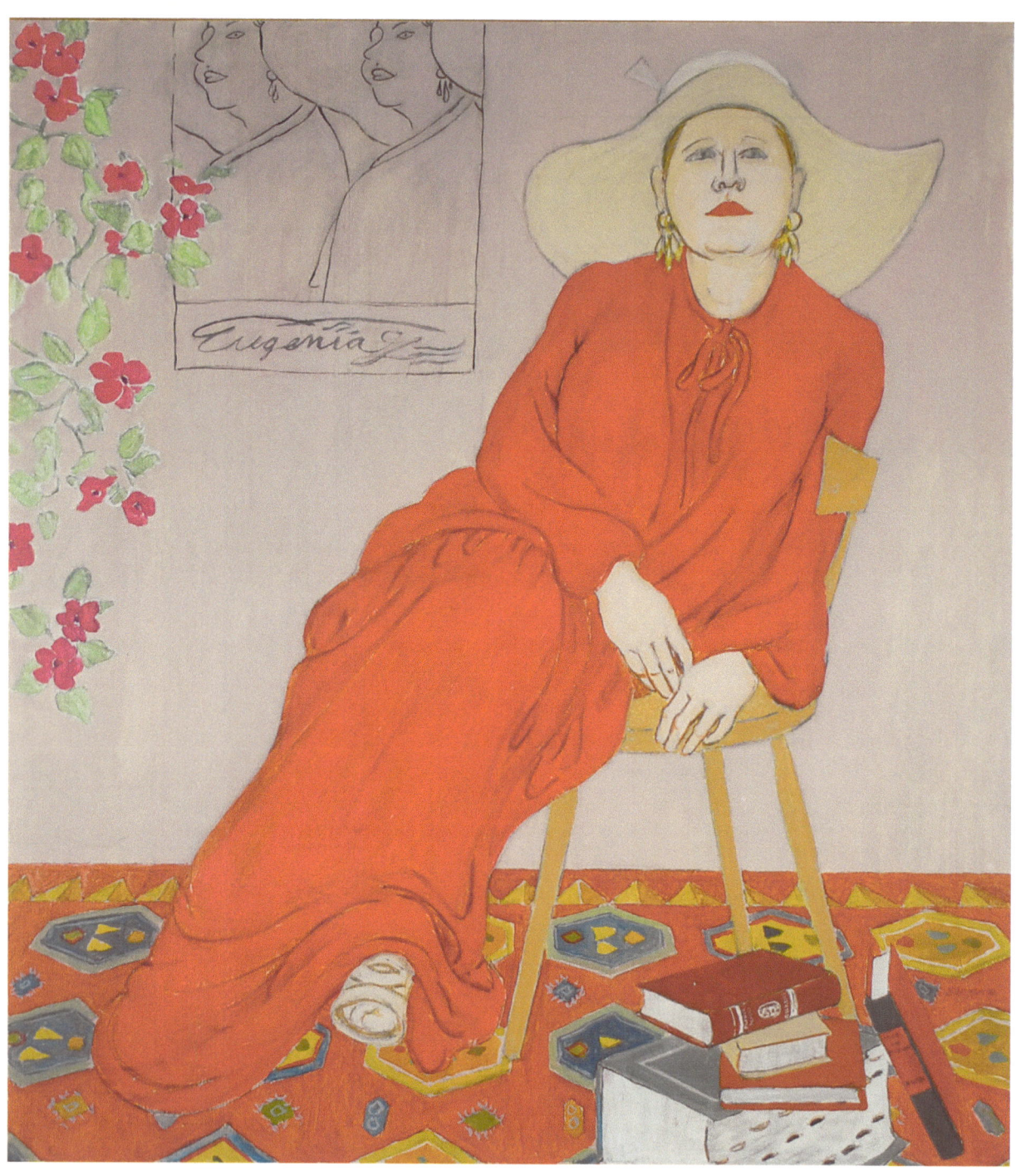

Eugenia Thornton, c. 1970
Acrylic on paper, 48 x 42 in.
ARTneo Collection, Gift of the artist, 2002-712

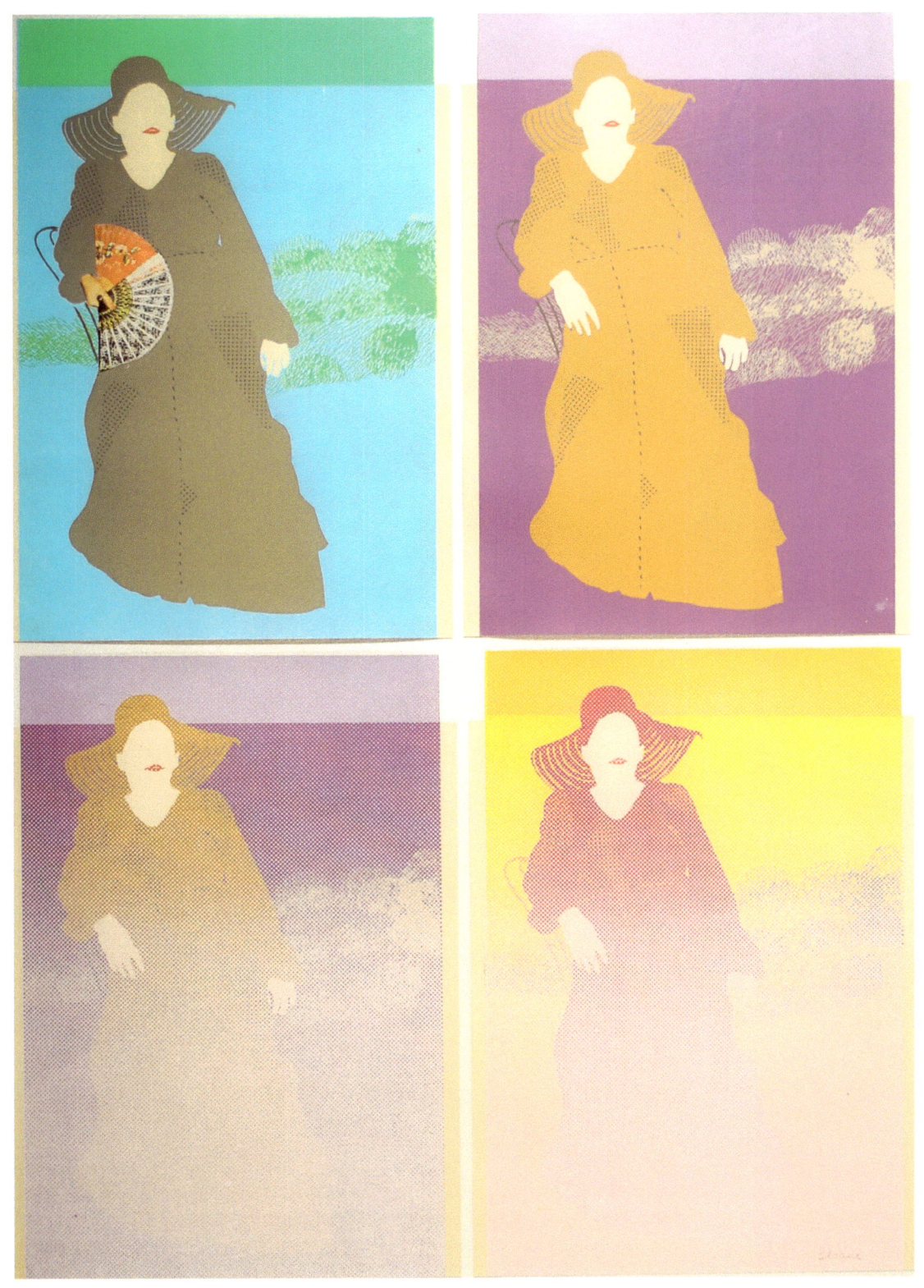

Eugenia Thornton, c. 1970
Screenprint on paper, 28 x 20.5 in.
ARTneo Collection, Gift of the artist, 2002-720

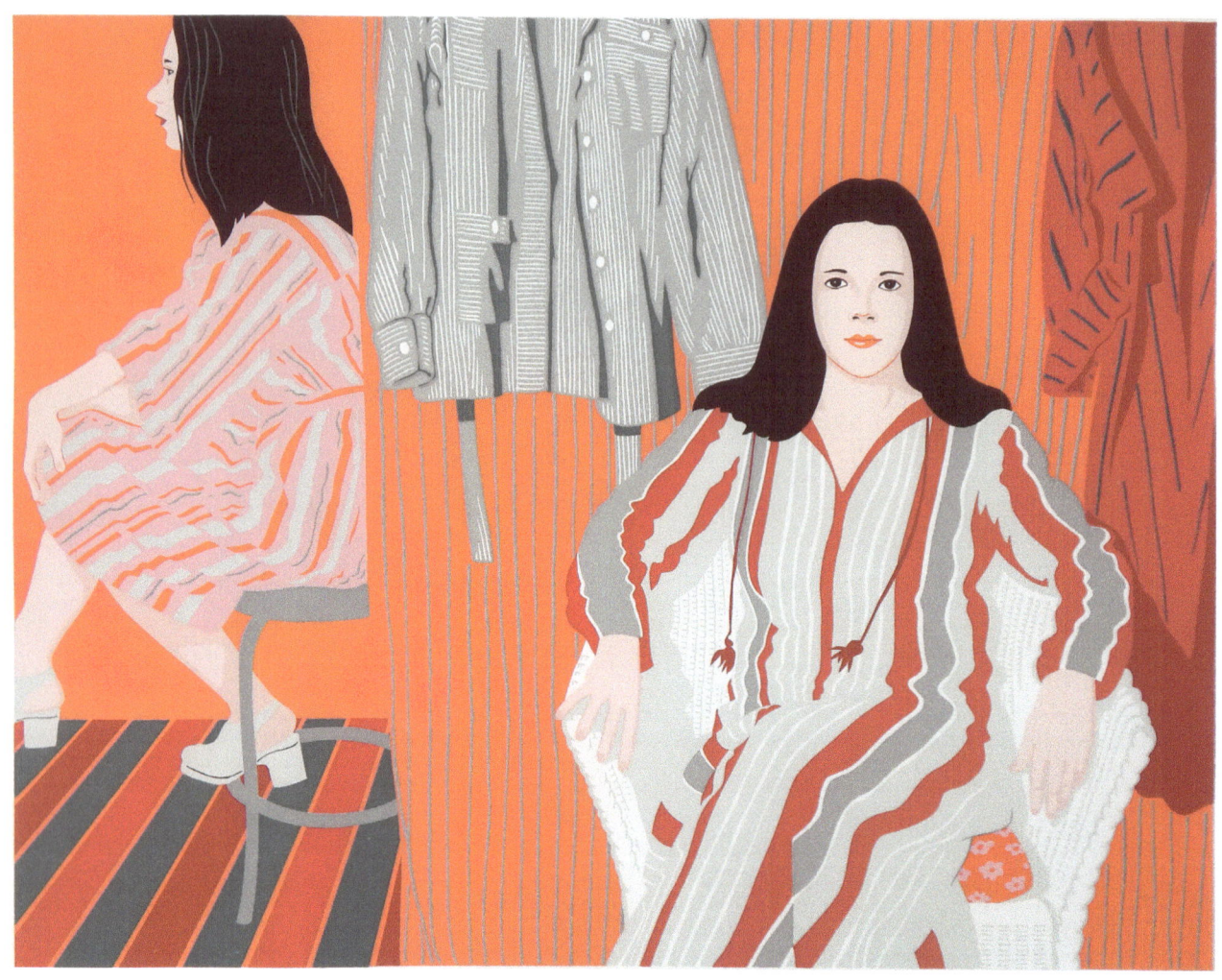

Women in Red Room, c. 1977
Screenprint on paper, 18 x 24 in.
Collection of Phyllis and Bob Lester

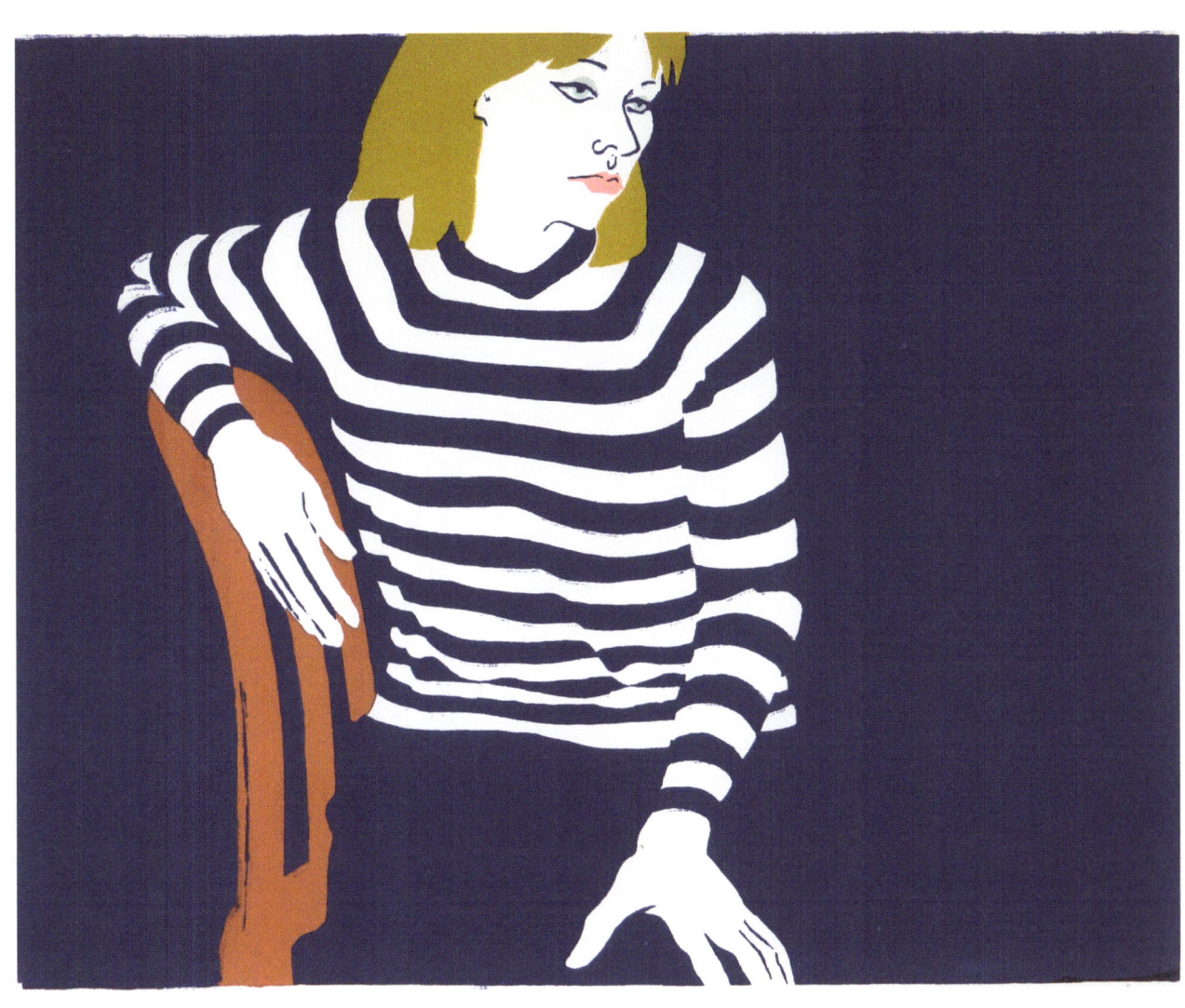

B.A., 1969
Screenprint on paper, 21 x 17 in.
ARTneo Collection, Gift of the artist, 2002-804

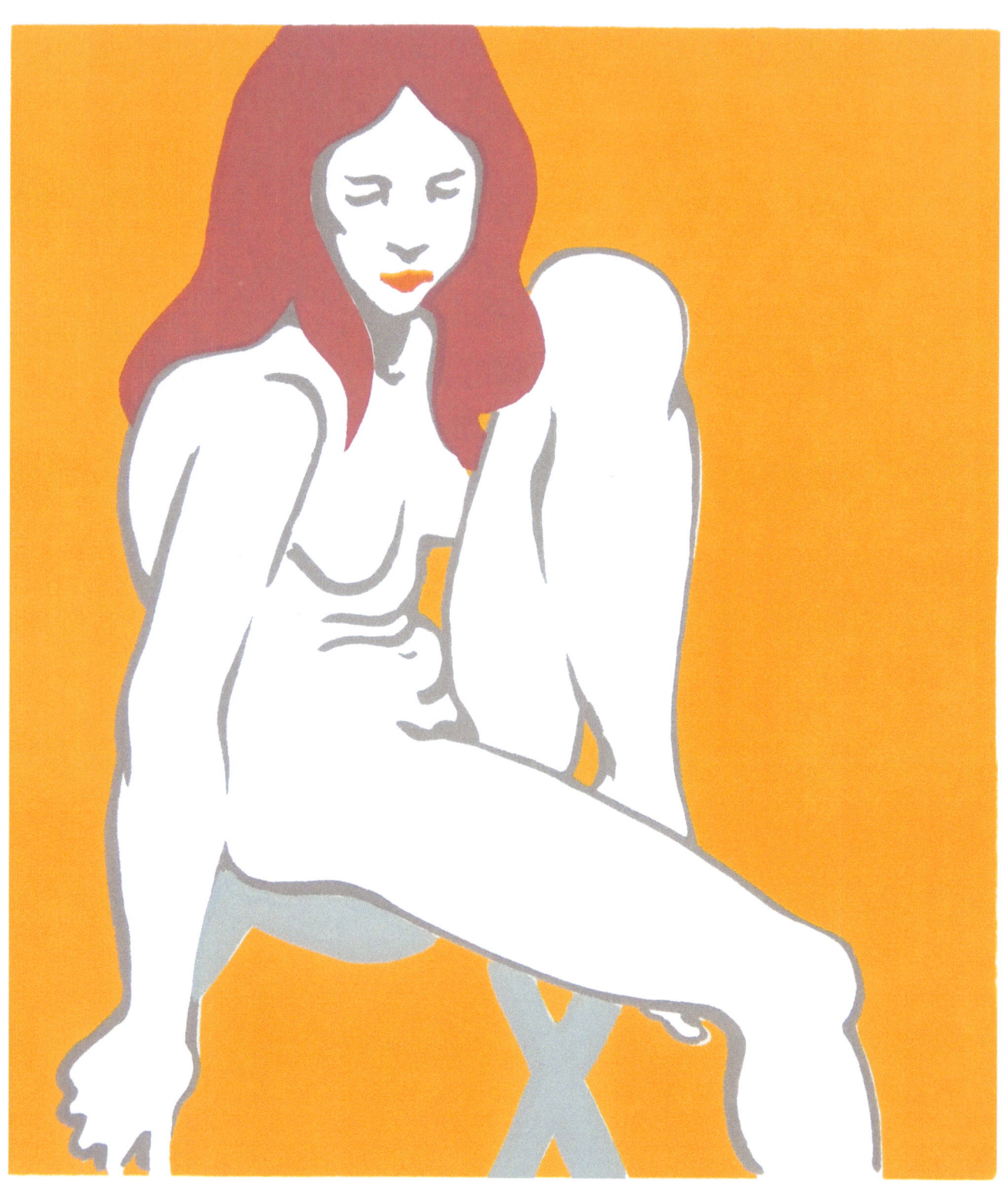

Untitled [Nude], 1973
Screenprint on paper, 7 x 6 in.
ARTneo Collection, Gift of the artist, 2002-771

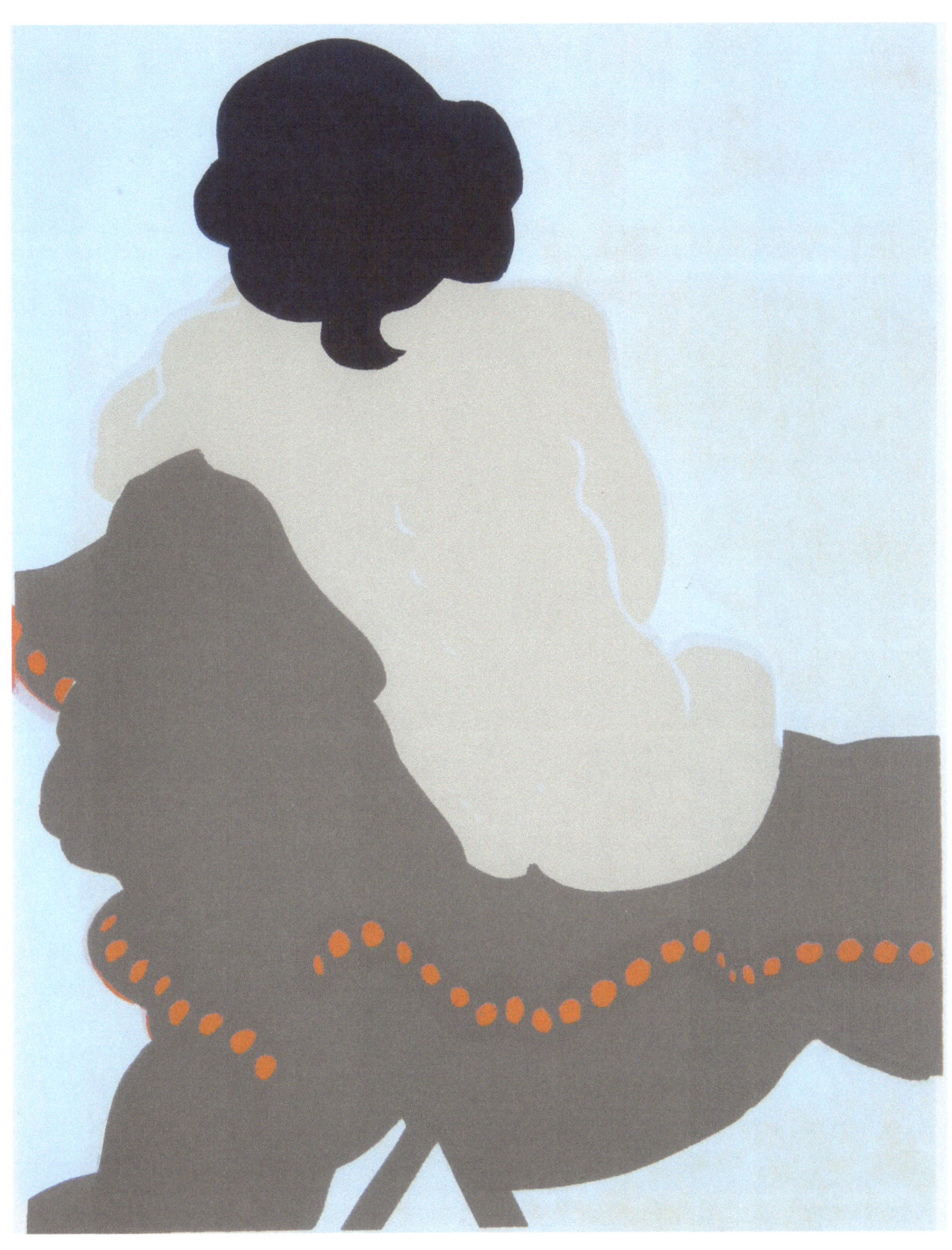

Untitled [Nude], 1973
Screenprint on paper, 8 x 6 in.
ARTneo Collection, Gift of the artist, 2002-772

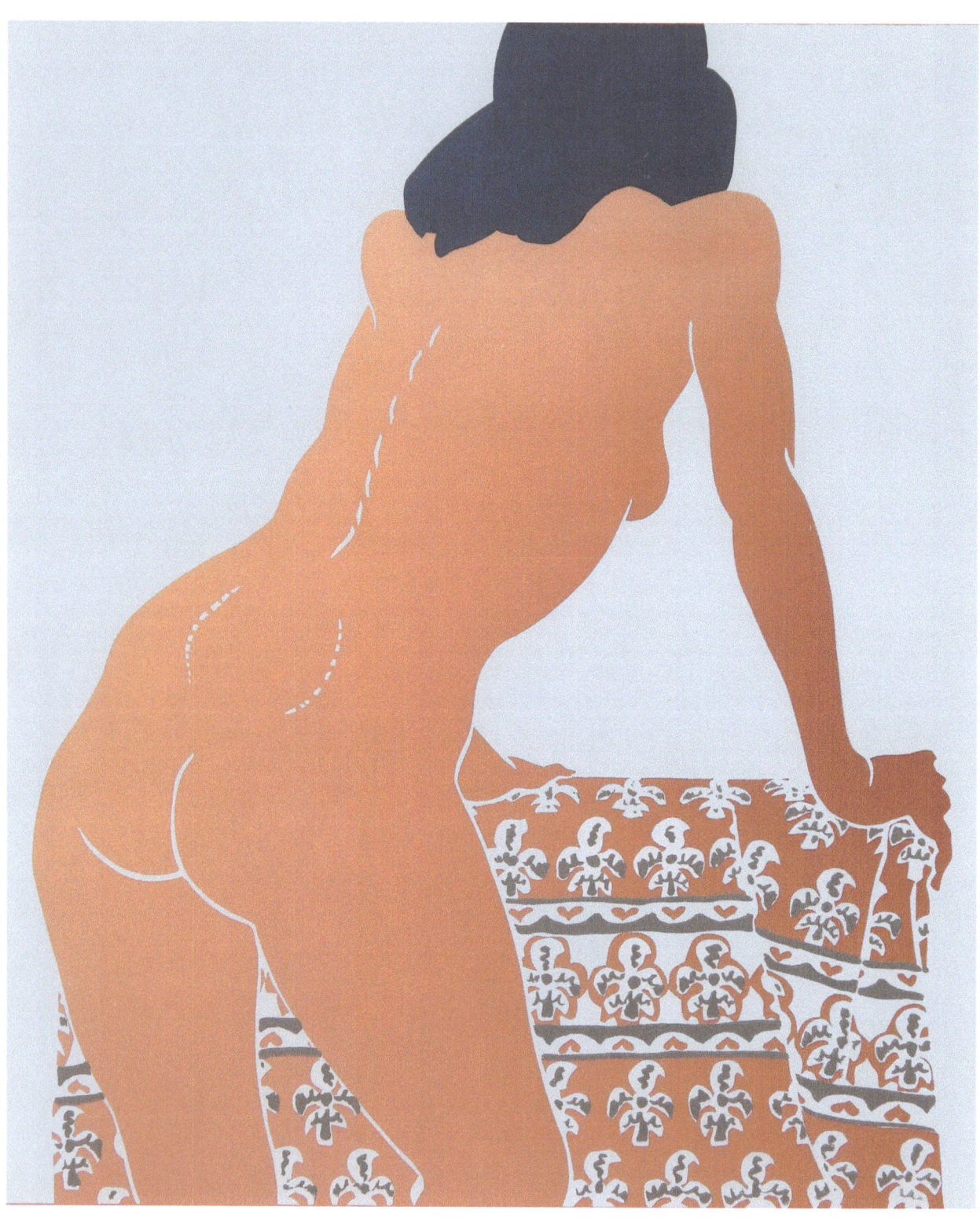

Nude Leaning, 1973
Screenprint on copper posterboard, 20.75 x 17 in.
ARTneo Collection, Gift of the artist, 2002-805

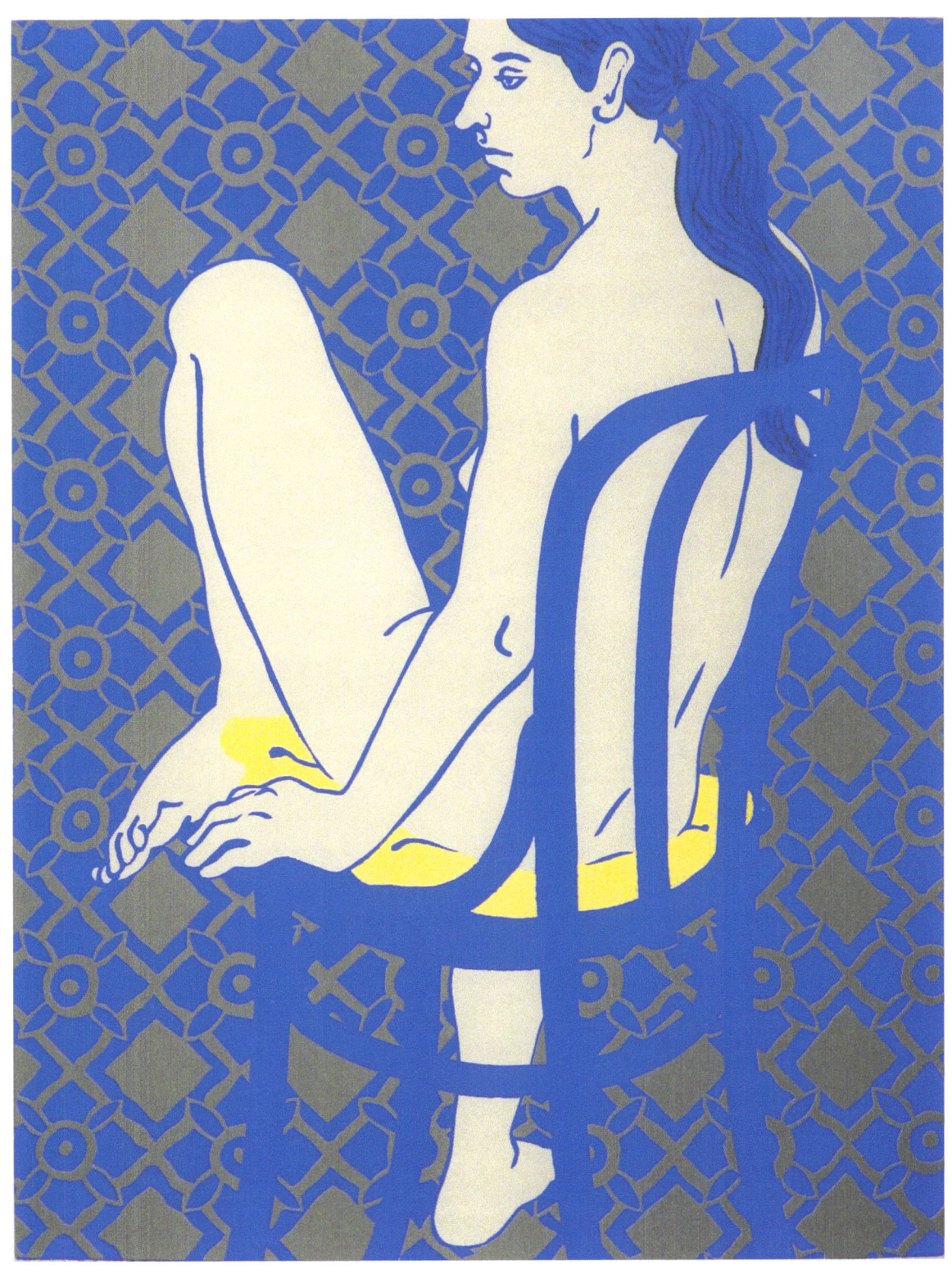

Nude on Blue Chair, 1973
Screenprint on paper, 21 x 16 in.
ARTneo Collection, Gift of the artist, 2002-803

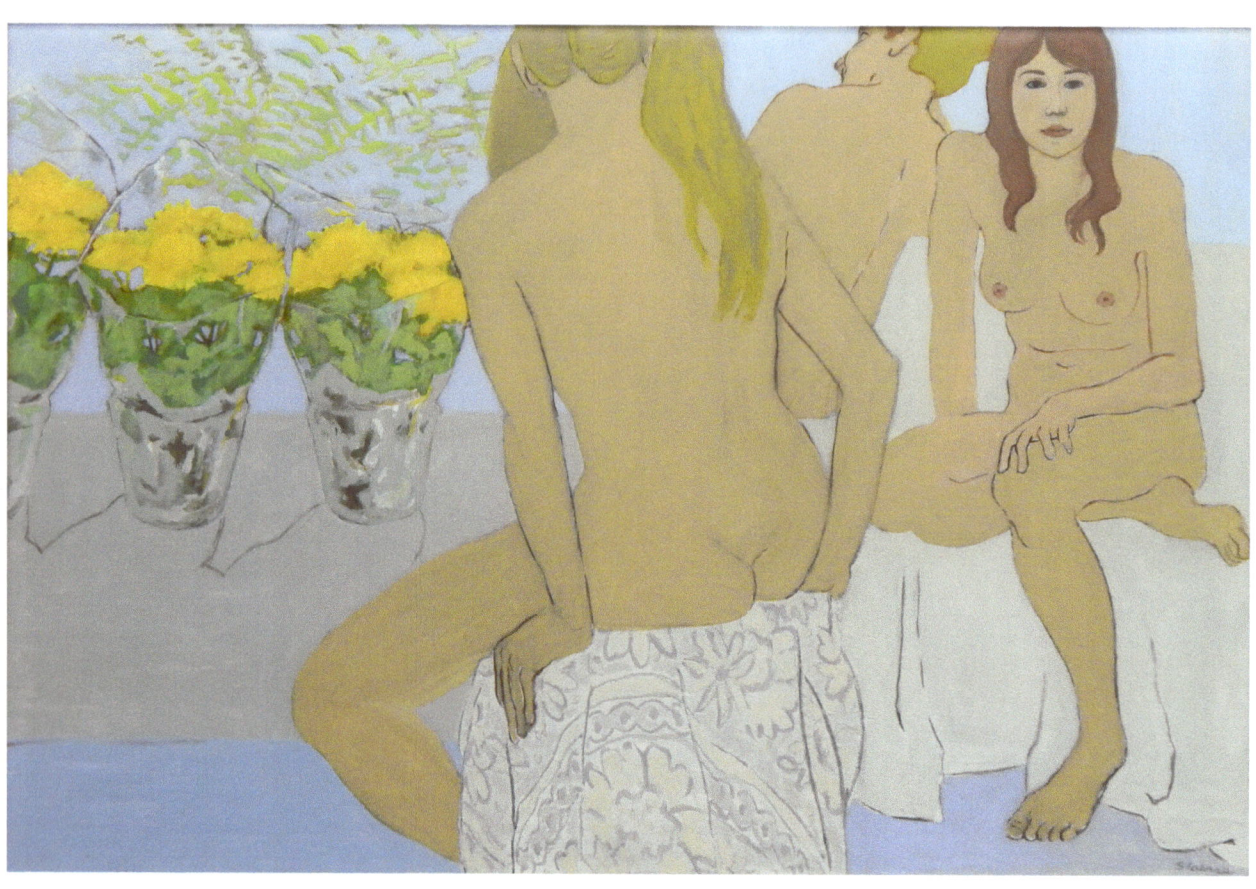

3 Nudes, 1973
Acrylic on canvas, 47 x 68 in.
Collection of Phyllis and Bob Lester

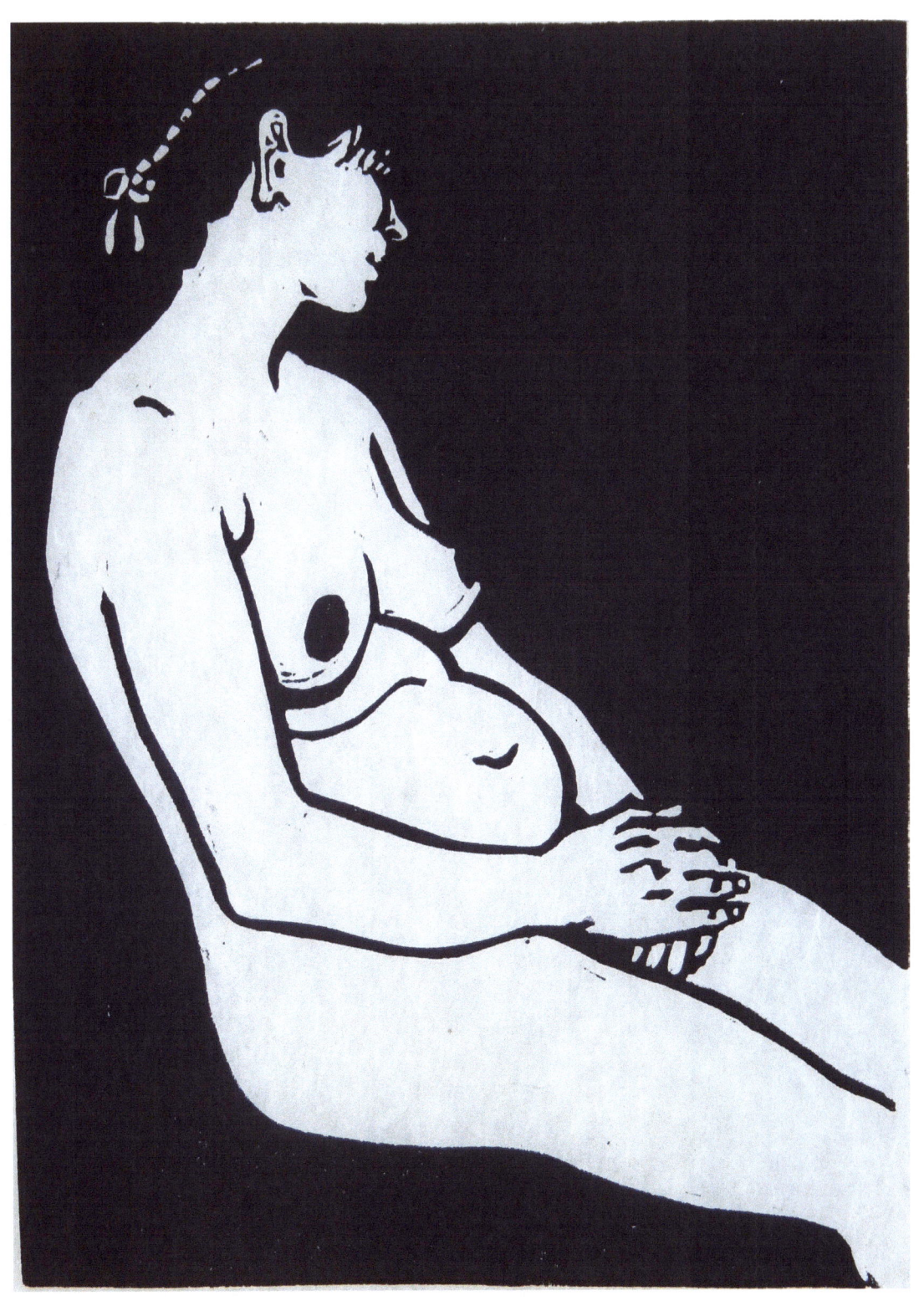

Seated Nude, 1970
Corkcut on paper, 17 x 12 in.
ARTneo Collection, Gift of the artist, 2002-813

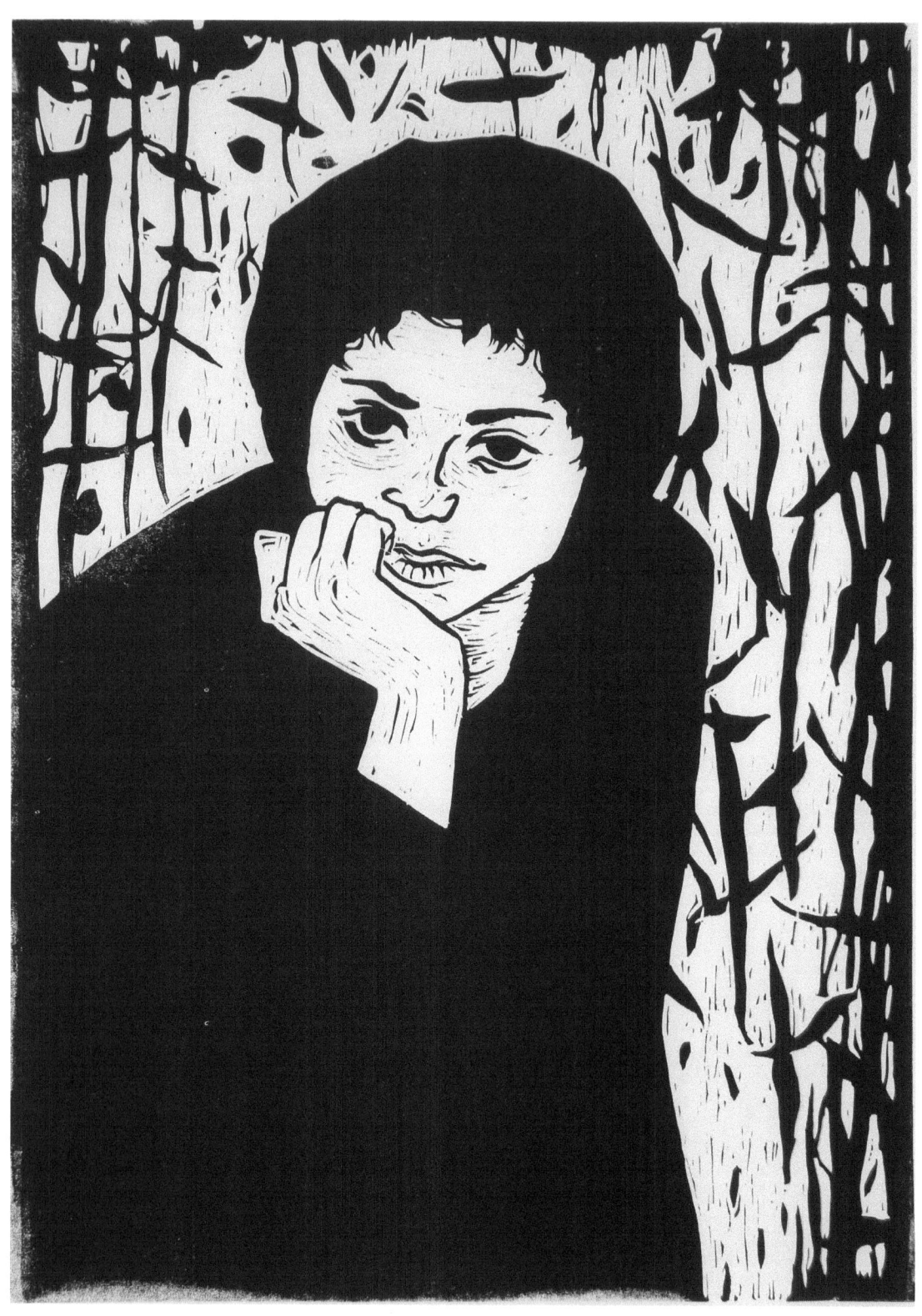

Self Portrait, 1960
Corkcut on paper, 22.5 x 15.5 in.
ARTneo Collection, Gift of the artist, 2002-794

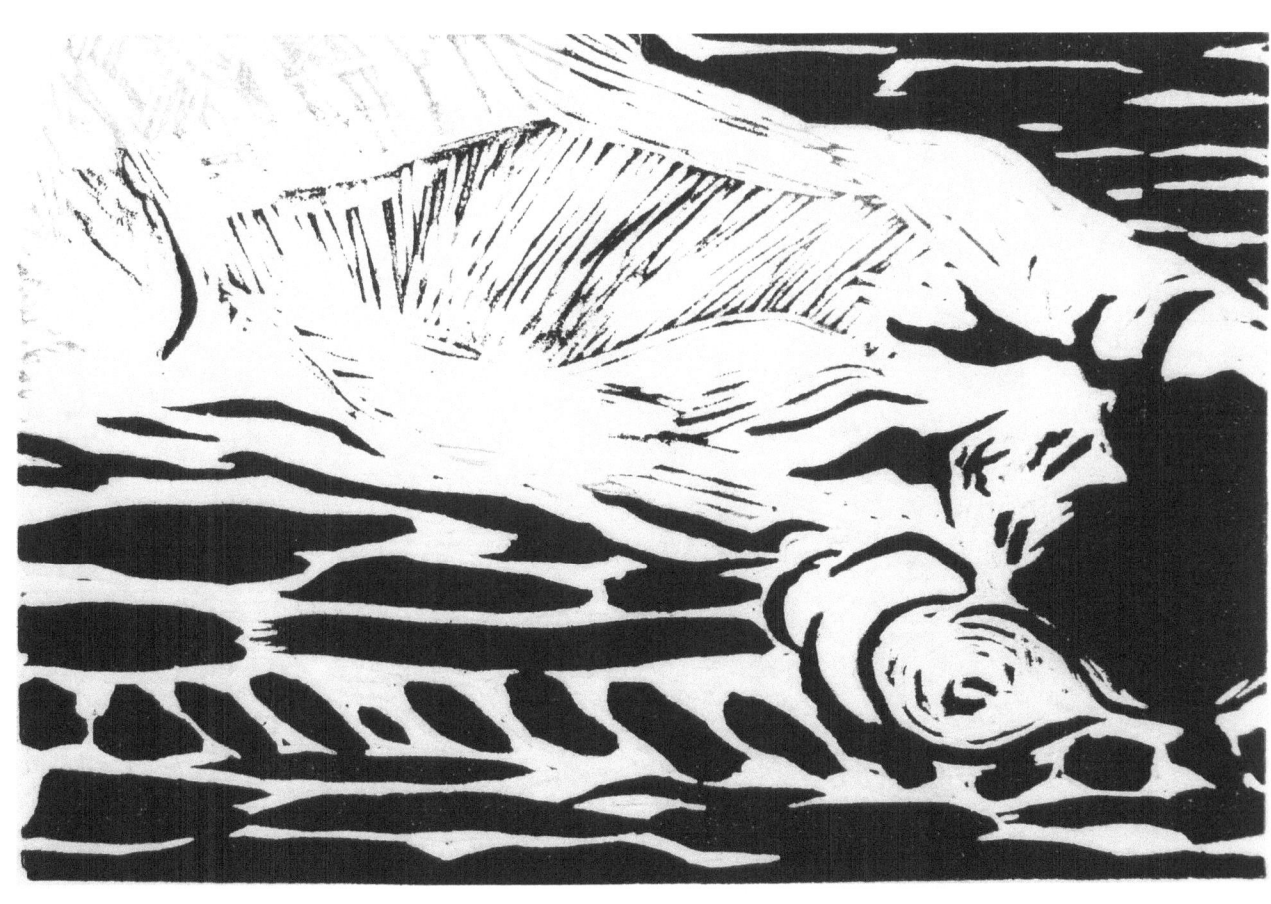

Ginna Resting, 1963
Corkcut on paper, 9 x 3.5 in.
ARTneo Collection, Gift of the artist, 2002-785

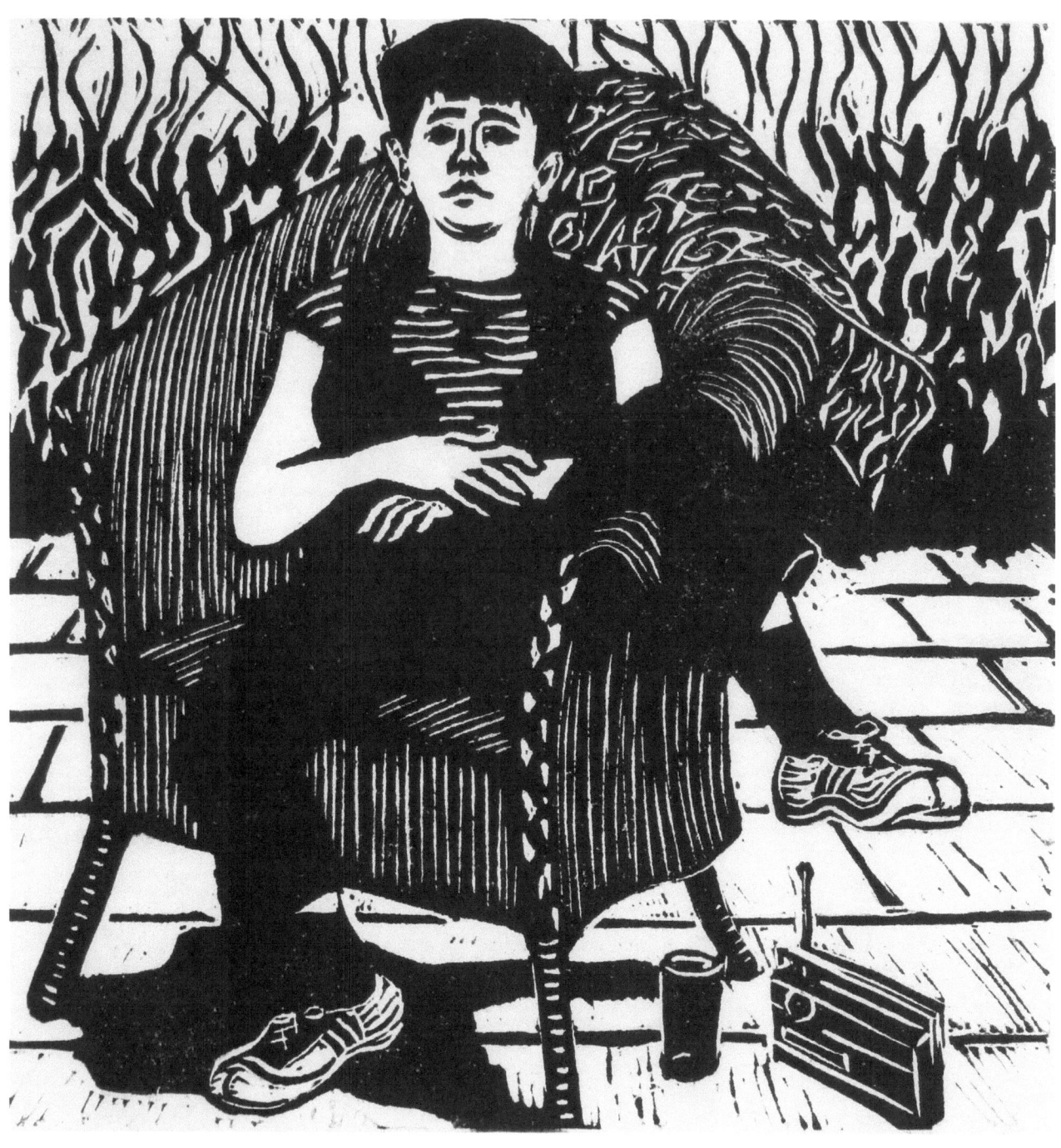

Hiram, 1970
Corkcut on paper, 12 x 11 in.
ARTneo Collection, Gift of the artist, 2002-773

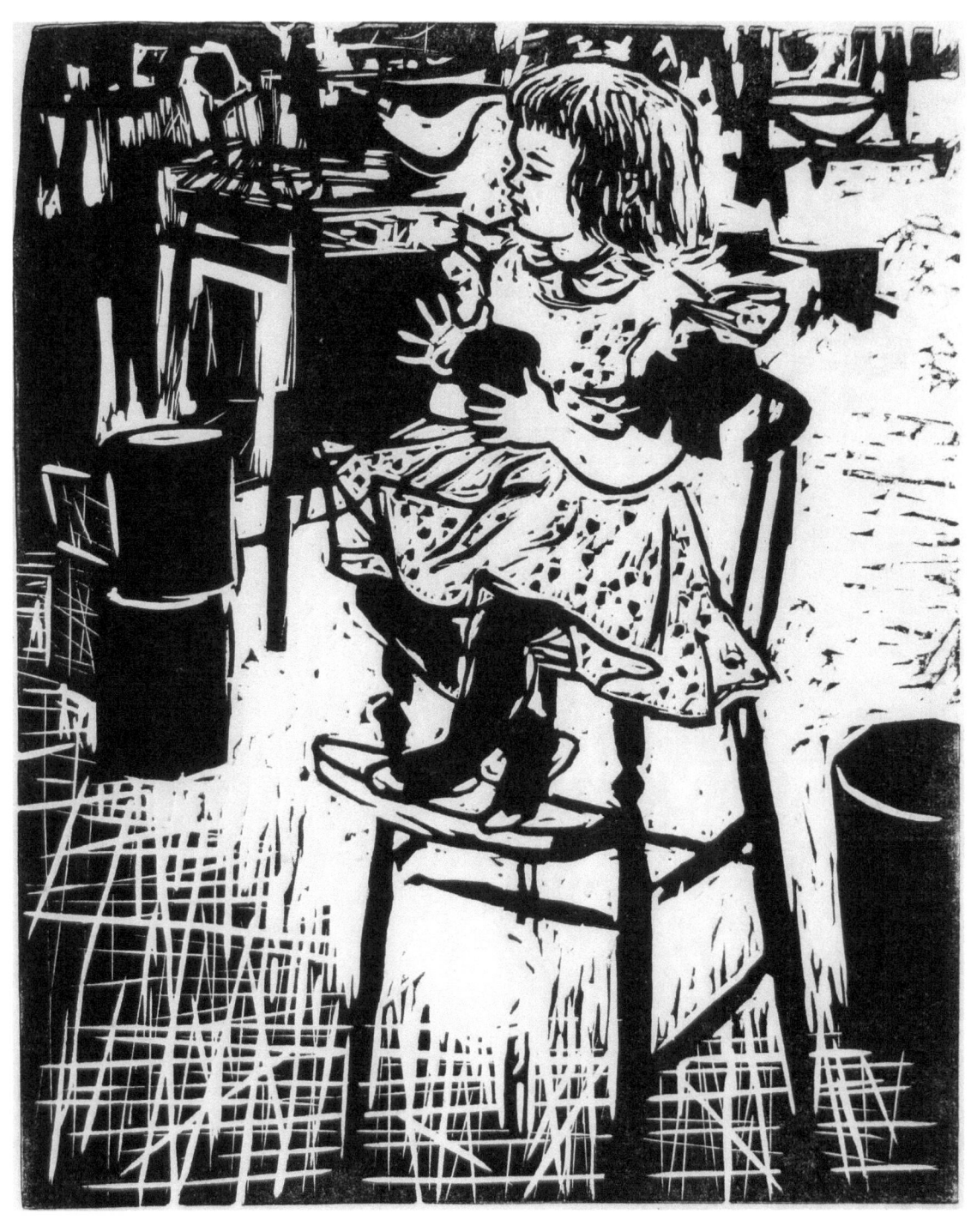

Lisa in Studio, 1961
Corkcut on paper, 10 x 8 in.
ARTneo Collection, Gift of the artist, 2002-783

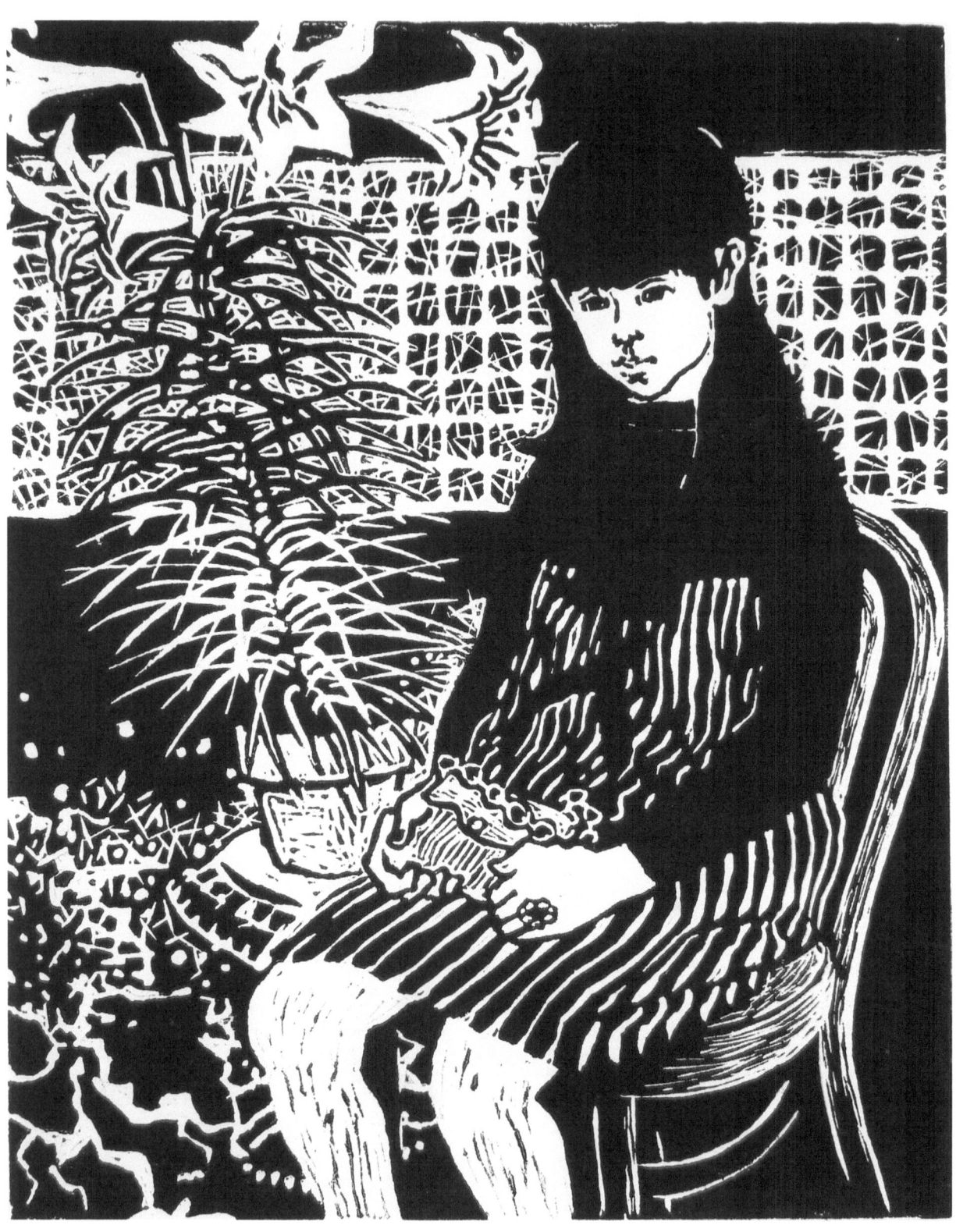

Lisa and Lillies, 1968
Corkcut on paper, 18.5 x 14.5 in.
ARTneo Collection, Gift of the artist, 2002-798

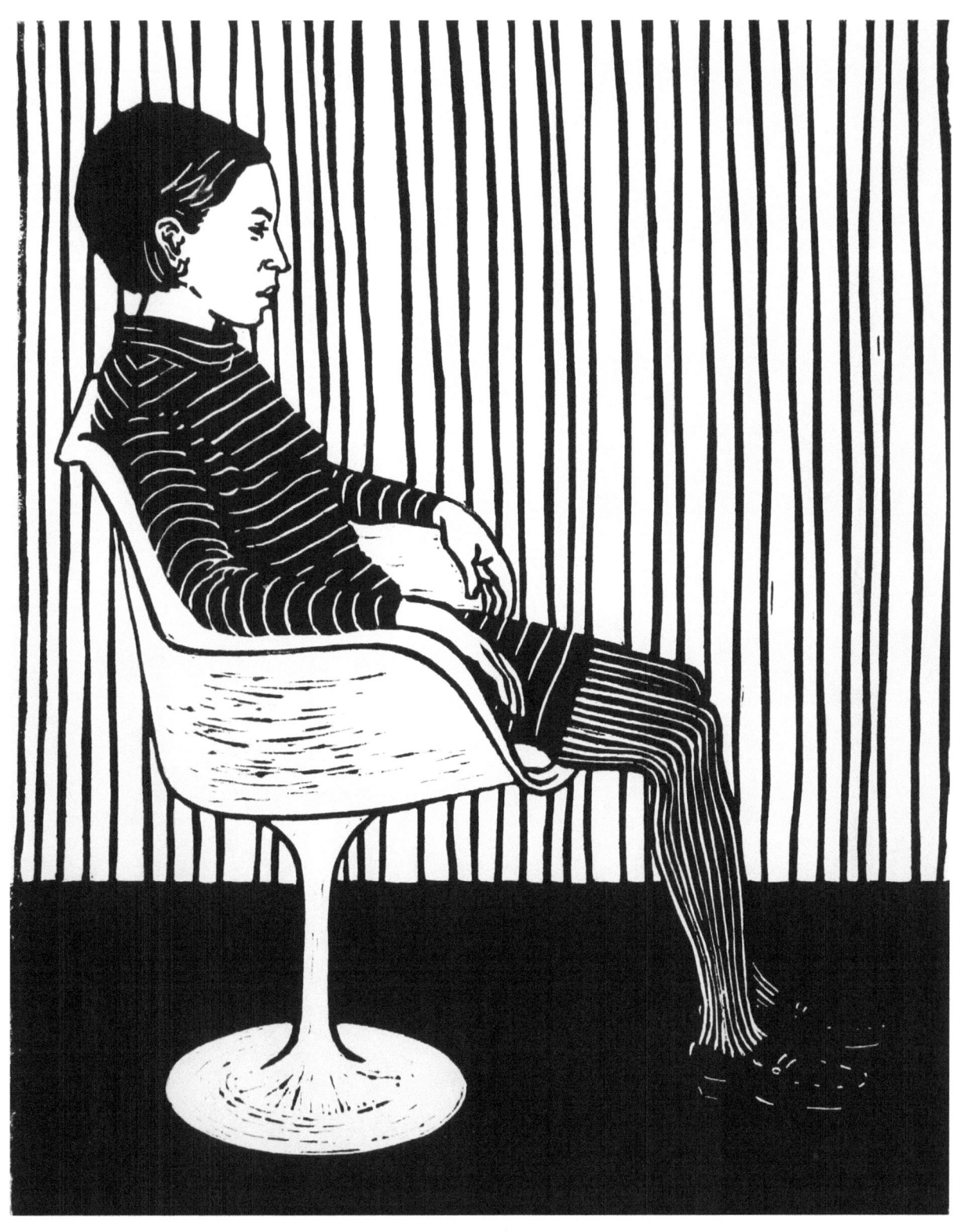

Naomi, 1969
Corkcut on paper, 20 x 15.75 in.
ARTneo Collection, Gift of the artist, 2002-795

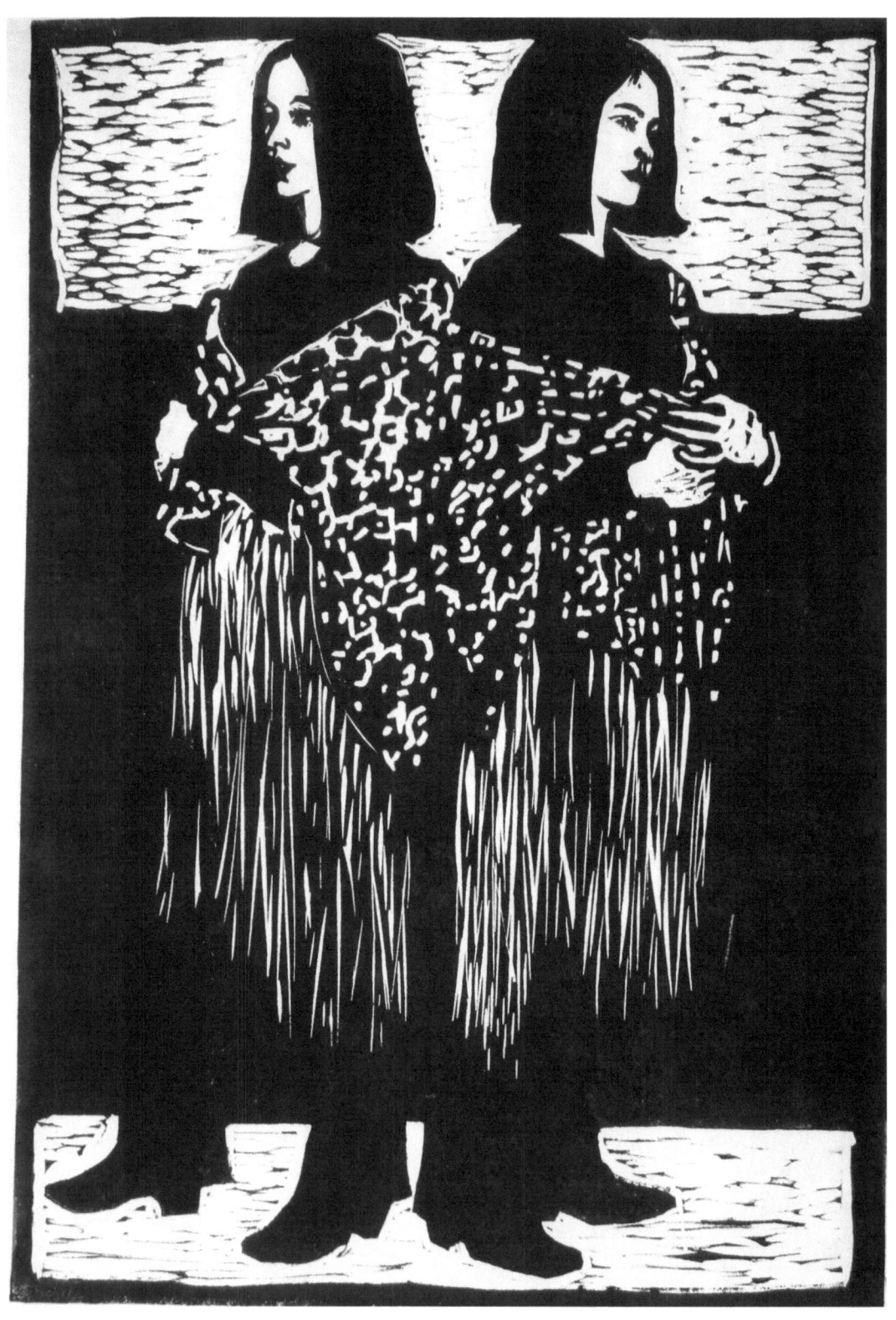

Ginna Times Two, 1970
Corkcut on paper, 23.5 x 15.75 in.
ARTneo Collection, Gift of the artist, 2002-814

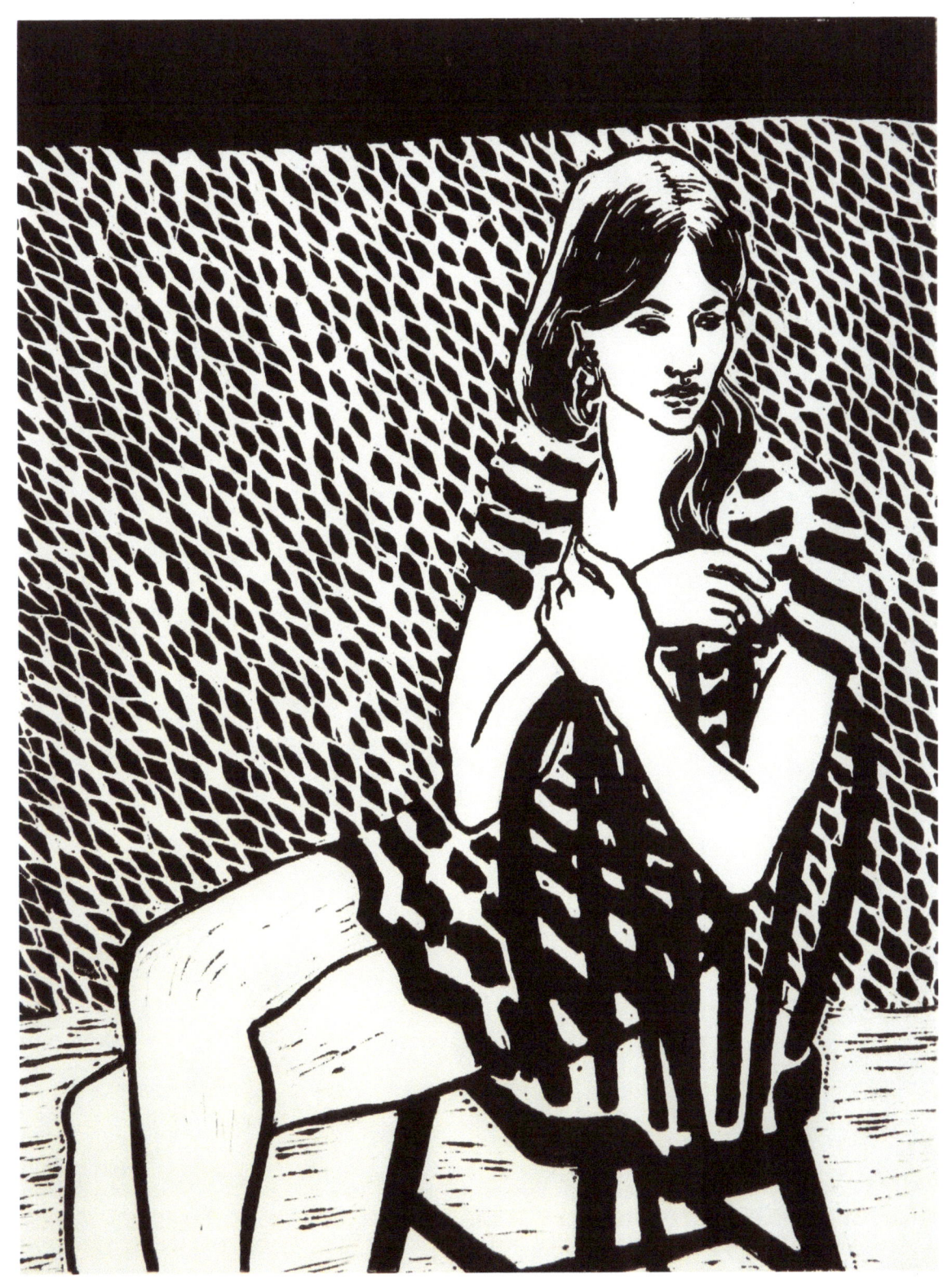

Sylvia, 1968
Corkcut on paper, 20 x 14 in.
ARTneo Collection, Gift of the artist, 2002-797

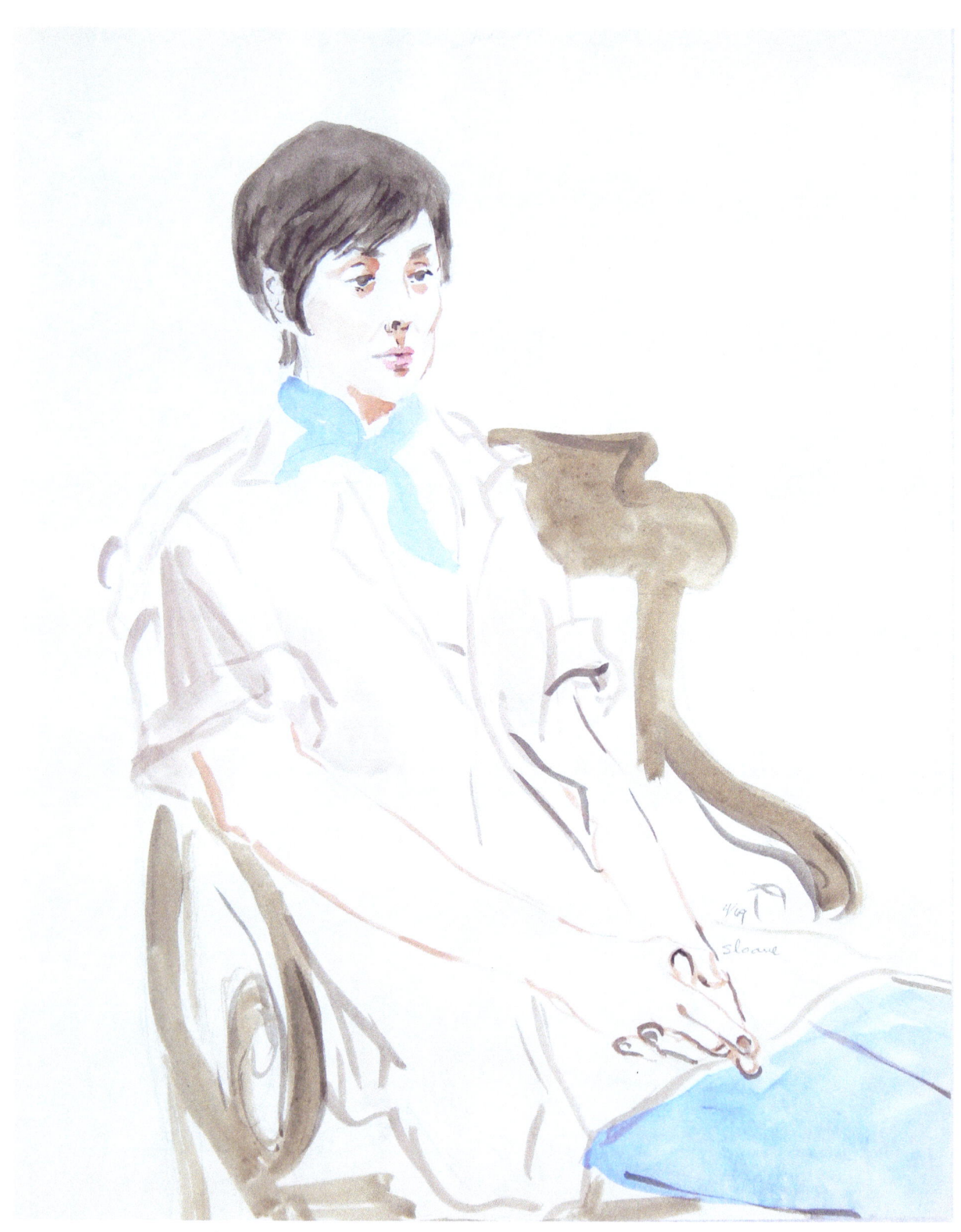

Untitled [portrait of a woman], 1969
Watercolor on paper, 17.5 x 13.75 in.
ARTneo Collection, Gift of the artist, 2002-770

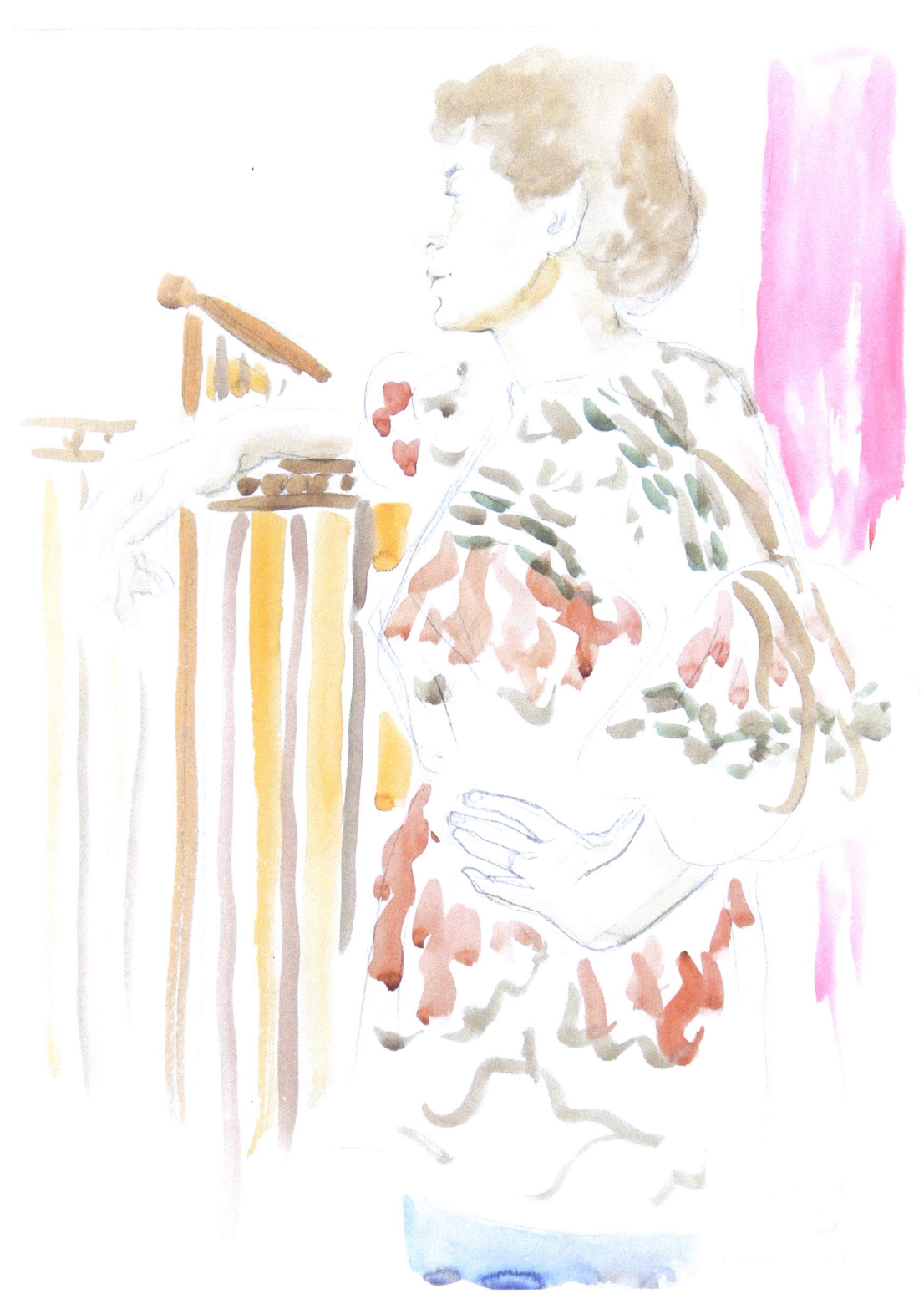

Elaine Cohen, 1969
Watercolor and graphite on paper, 23 x 17 in.
ARTneo Collection, Gift of the artist, 2002-808

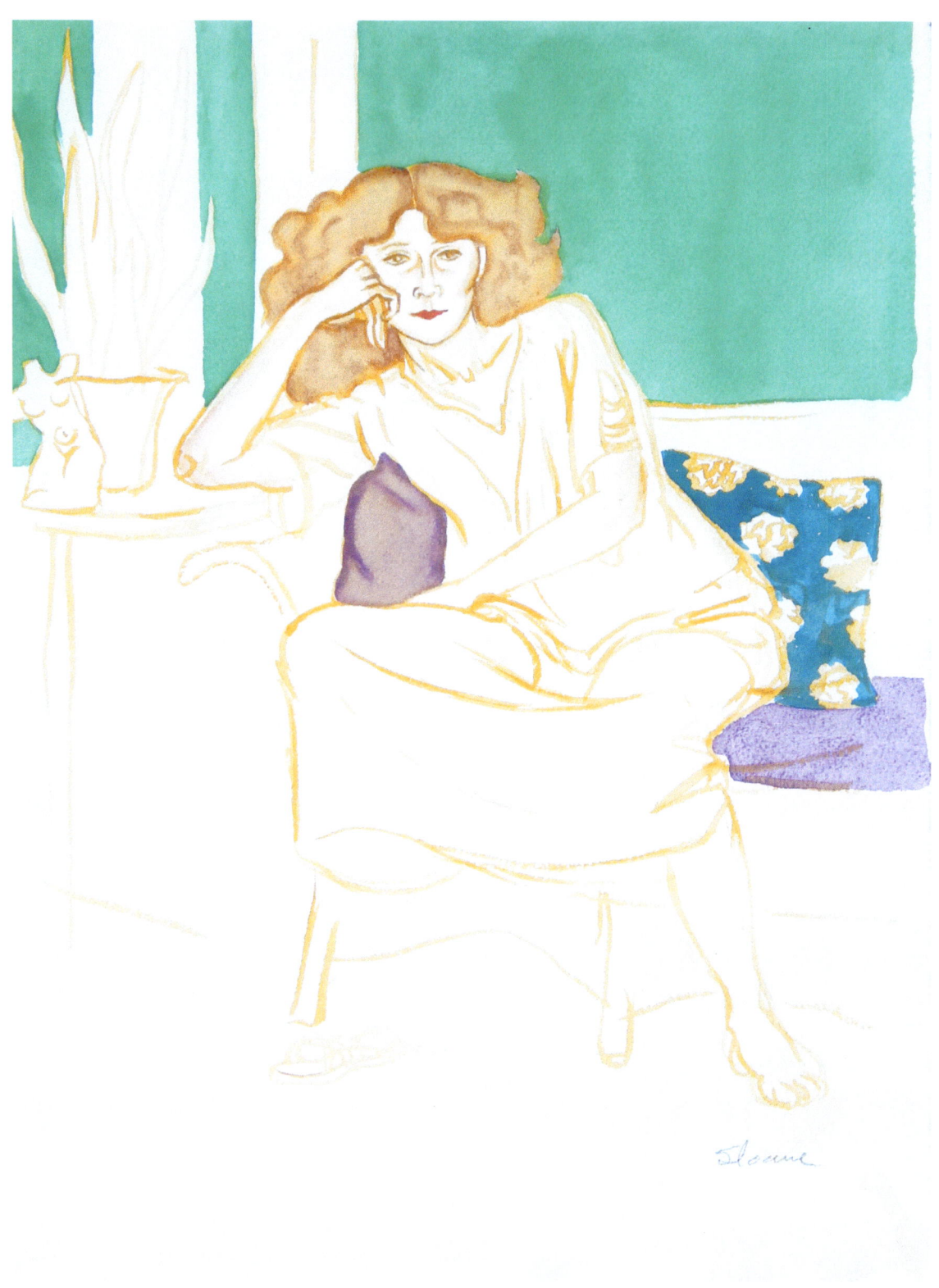

Untitled [portrait of a woman], c. 1970
Watercolor on paper, 15 x 11 in.
ARTneo Collection, Gift of the artist, 2002-782

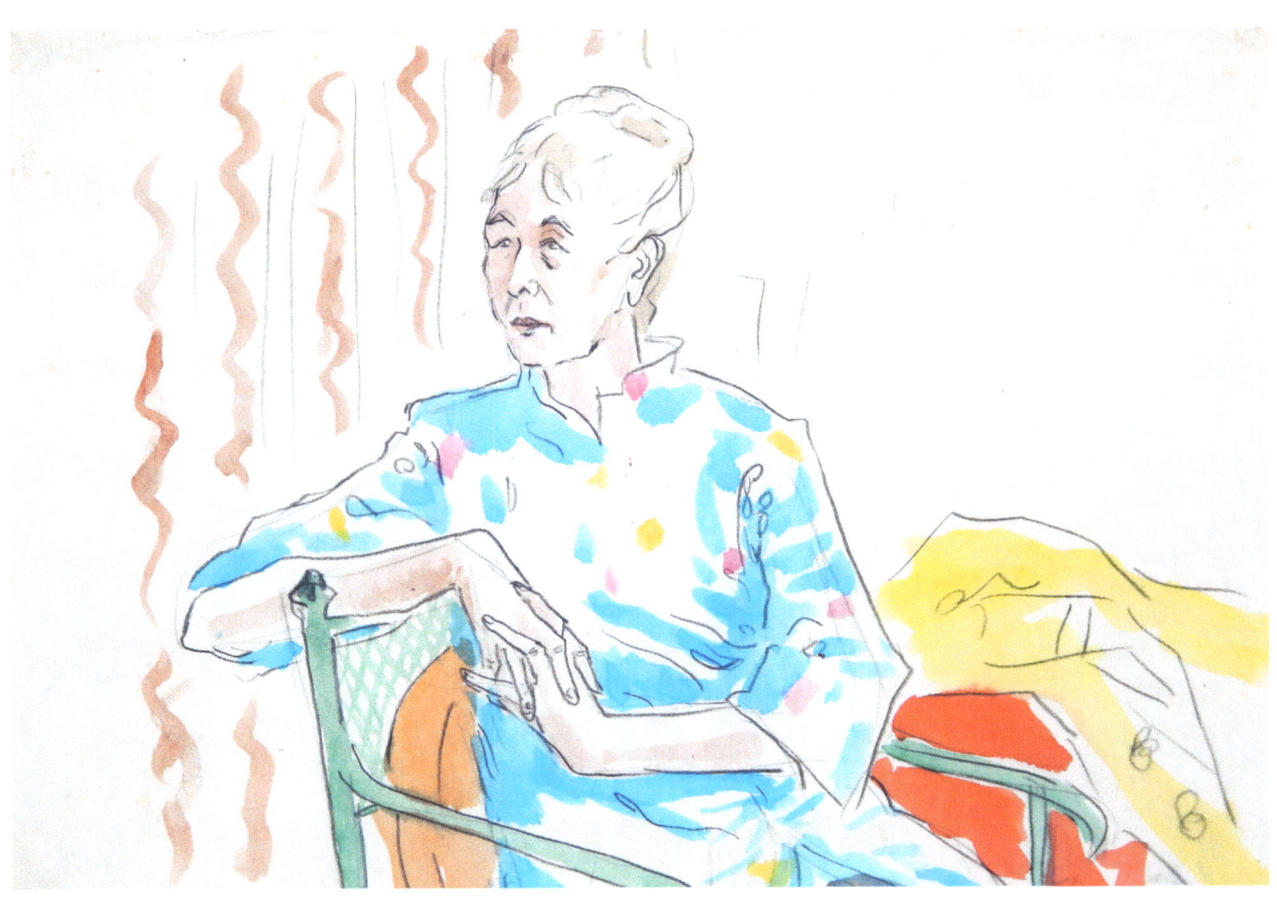

Eleanor Frampton, c. 1970
Watercolor and graphite on paper, 17 x 23 in.
ARTneo Collection, Gift of the artist, 2002-816

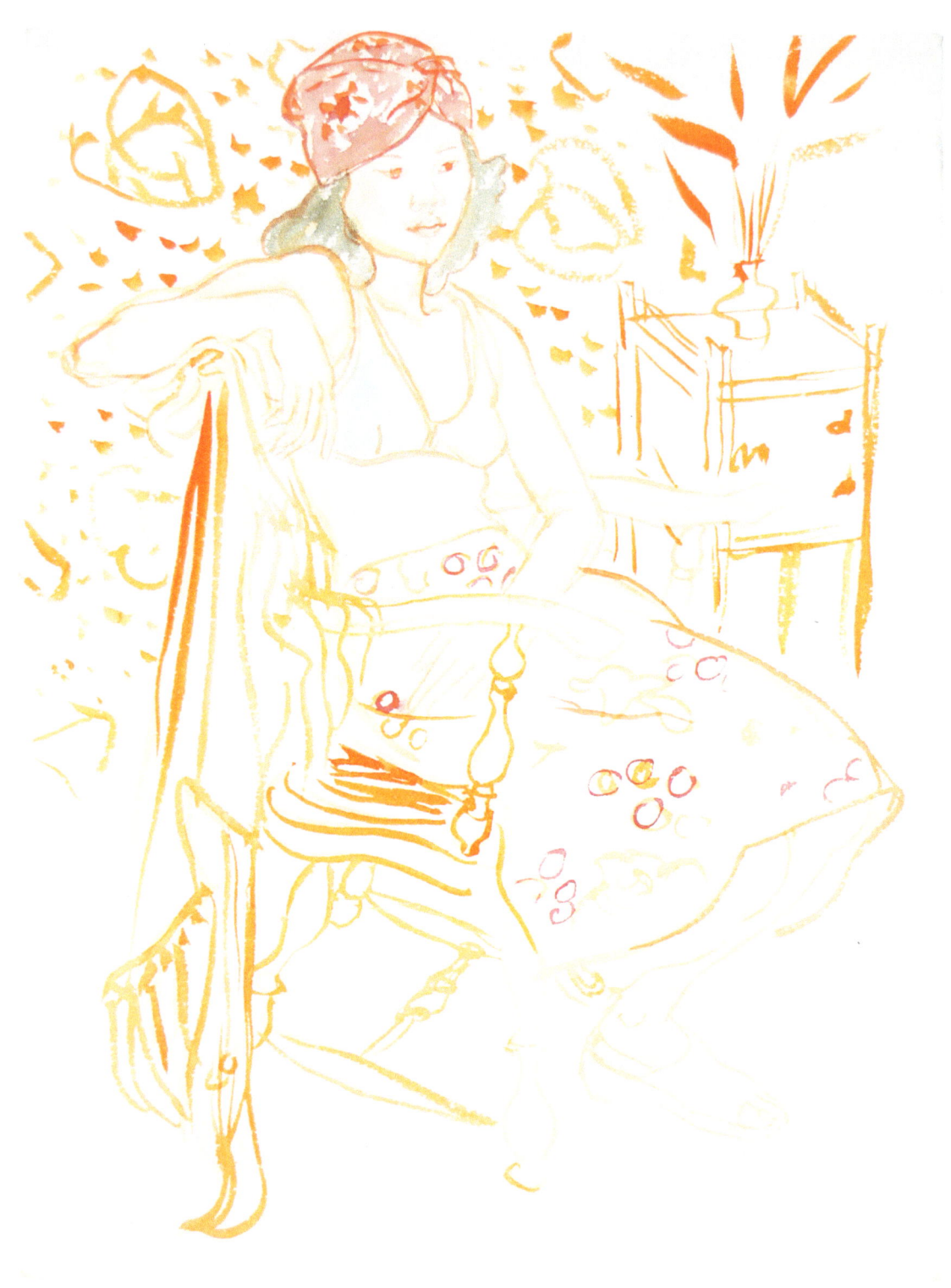

Untitled [portrait of a woman], c. 1970
Watercolor on paper, 15.25 x 11 in.
ARTneo Collection, Gift of the artist, 2002-779

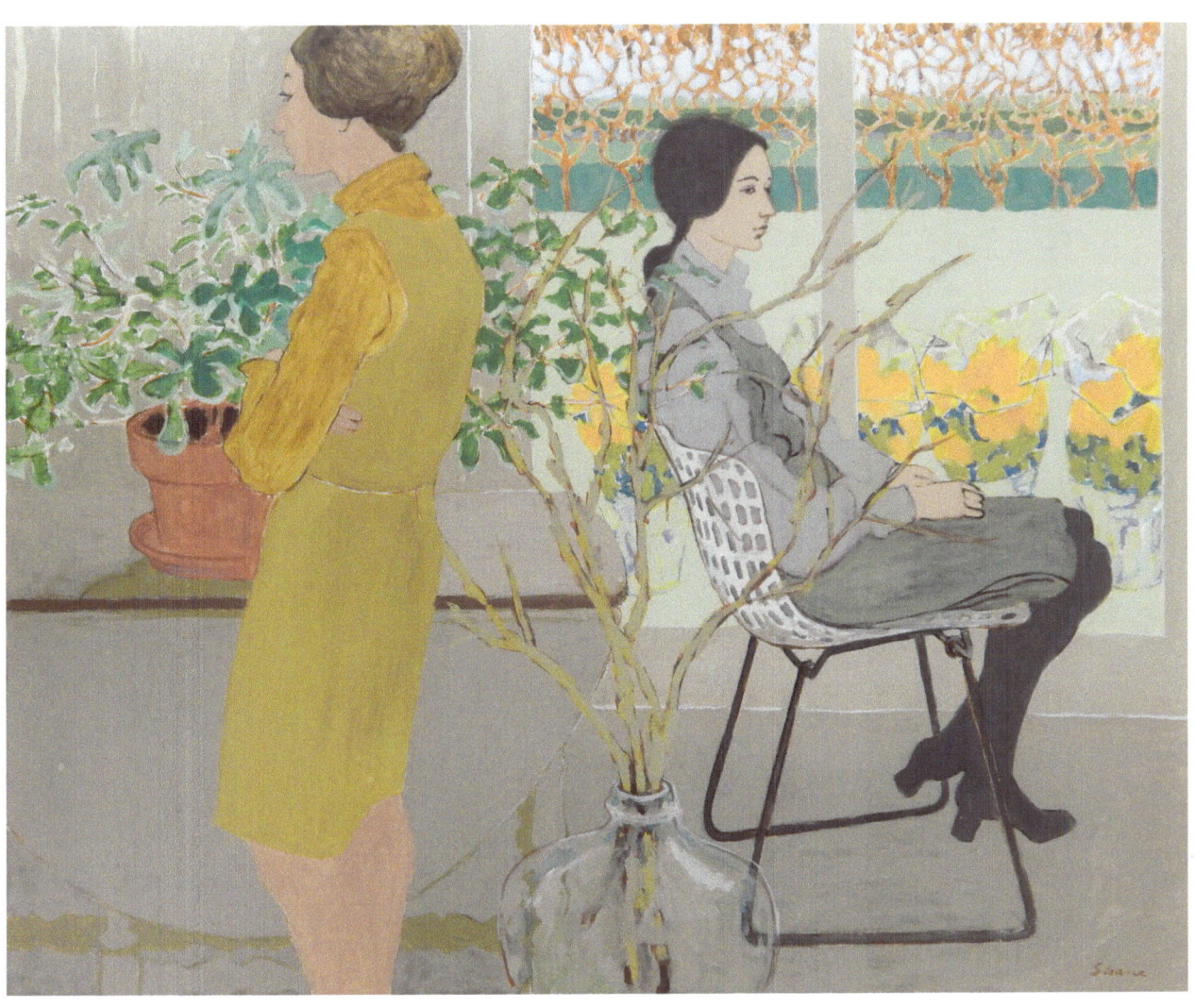

Barbara, c. 1975
Acrylic on canvas, 52 x 64.5 in.
Collection of Phyllis and Bob Lester

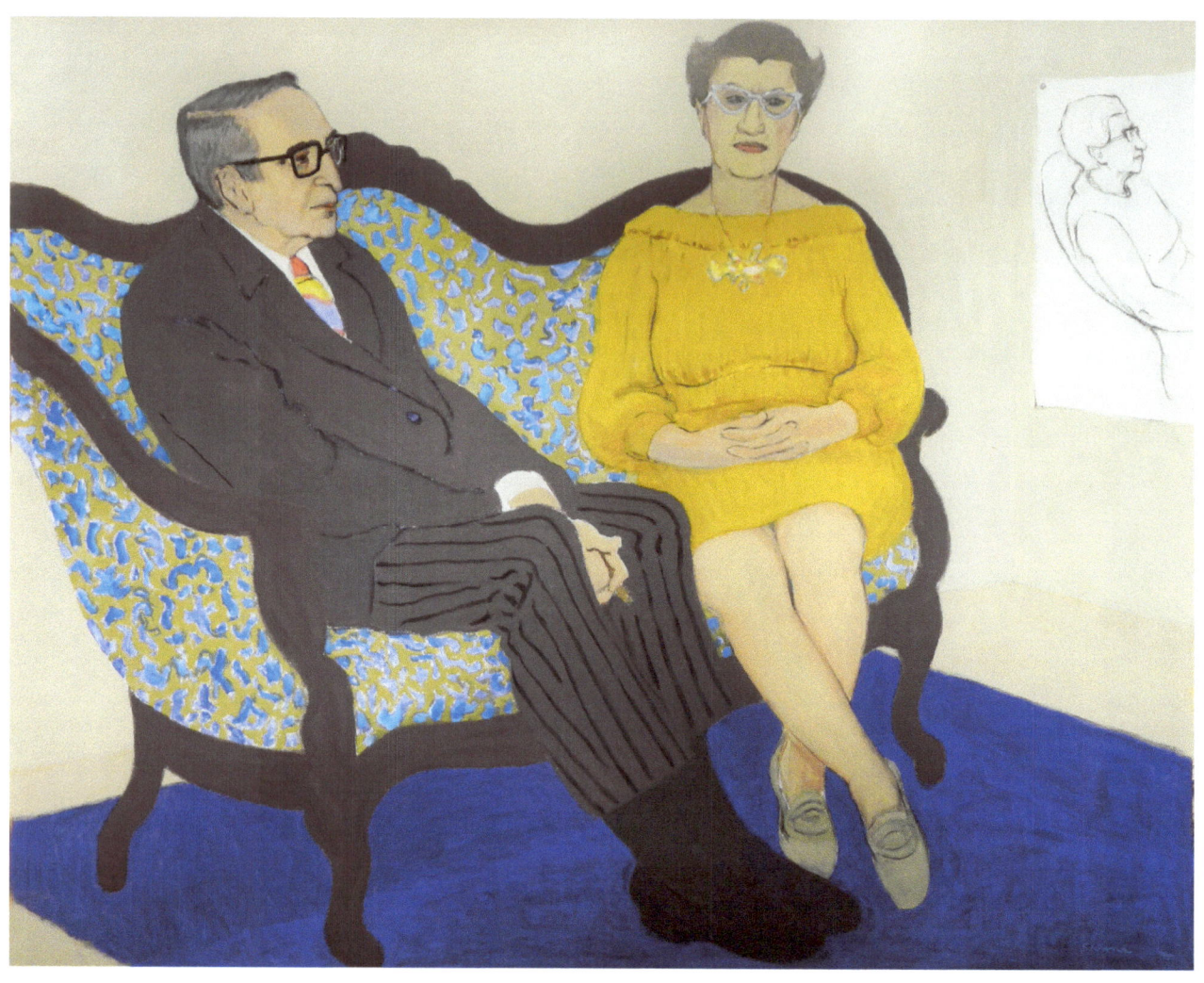

Henry and Lillian Steinberg, c. 1973
Acrylic on canvas, 52 × 64 in.
ARTneo Collection, Gift of the artist, 2002-711

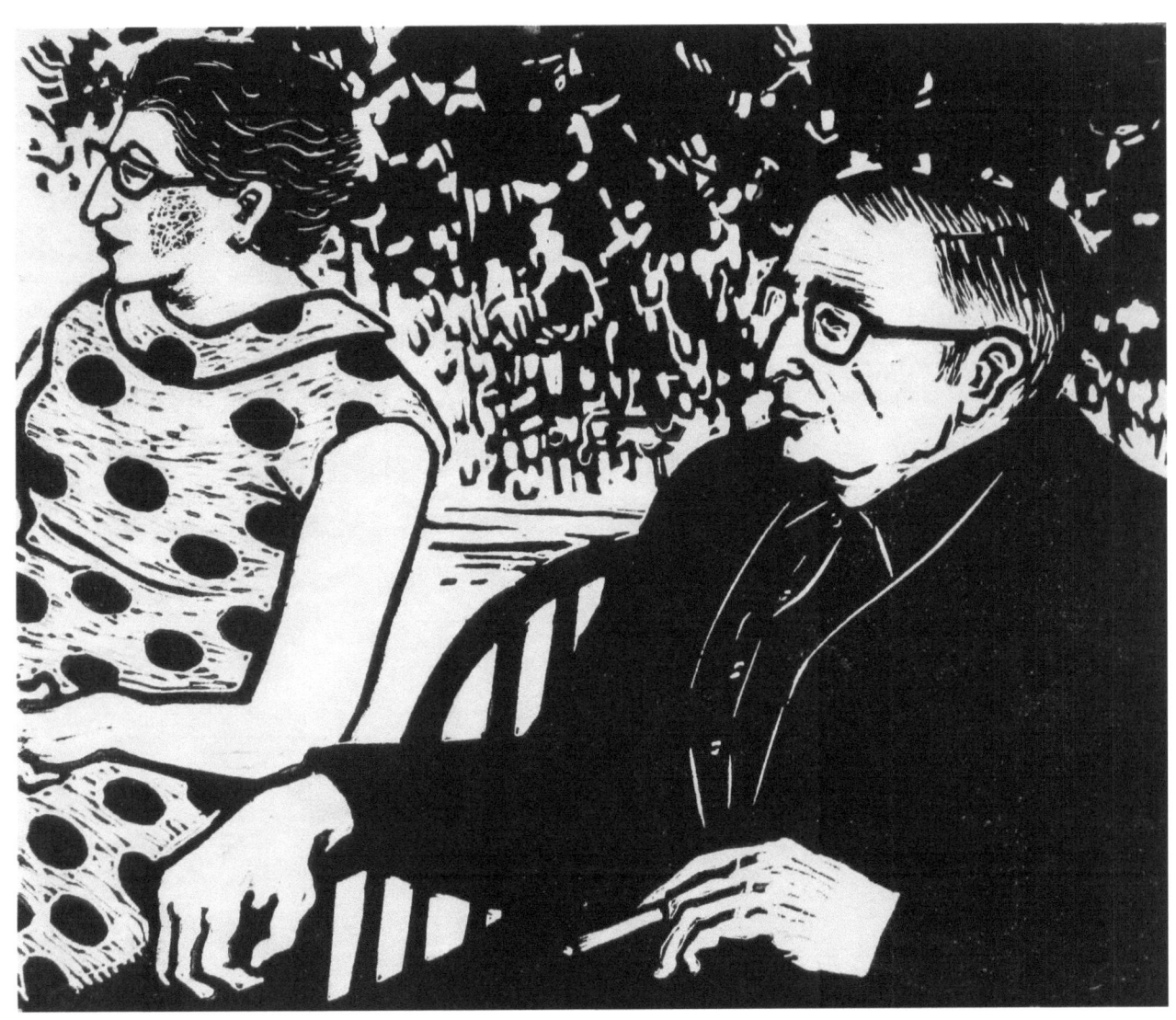

The Steinbergs, 1970
Woodcut on Paper, 12.625 x 14.625 in.
ARTneo Collection, Gift of the artist, 1986-253